To Bet...

May yours...

never stop growing closer

To Christ. Gail MacDonald

Mt. 12:34

12/03

A HEART FOR THE MASTER

A Heart for the Master
120 Devotional Readings

GORDON AND GAIL MACDONALD

VINE BOOKS
SERVANT PUBLICATIONS
ANN ARBOR, MICHIGAN

Vine Books is an imprint of Servant Publications especially designed to serve
evangelical Christians.

Published by Servant Publications
P.O. Box 8617
Ann Arbor, MI 48107

Cover Design: Brian Fowler-DesignTeam, Grand Rapids, Michigan

00 01 02 03   10 9 8 7 6 5 4 3 2 1

Printed in the United States of America
ISBN 1-56955-189-8

Dedication

As we ponder the pathways of our spiritual journey, there is one group of fellow travelers that stand out and make it seem so worthwhile. These are the men and women of a younger generation in whose lives we have tried to make a difference. They know who they are. They have been in our home, they have been on the road with us, they have been there when the learning experiences came fast and quick. We held nothing back from them if it was ours to give. We love them and find our joy in what they are becoming.

To them this book of thoughts is dedicated with the prayer that they would have hearts for the Master. We are always excited and satisfied when they bring back reports to us of the ways in which God is alive and working in their lives.

Acknowledgements

Two gifted women have helped make *A Heart for the Master* a reality:

- Heidi Saxton, who went out of her way to enter our lives and suggest that we work together on this project. Among her many gifts is that of encouragement.

- Amy Deardorff, who has an editorial eye for a turn of word and phrase which makes a writer look and sound far better than he/she could ever have been alone.

To these special people and to the rest of the Servant Publications team we say a warm thank you for all your kindnesses.

Gail and Gordon MacDonald

Introduction

This book appears in the fortieth year of our marriage. During those four decades, one of the most important things we have learned is that every day ought to be marked by quiet periods. It is during these quiet times that we need to engage (individually and together) with the Master for purposes of worship, repentance, redirection, assurance, and inner vitality.

Both of us would be quick to confess that there have been times when we have not had (in the words of the book title) "A heart for the Master." In more youthful days, we were, like most others, full of energy, ambition, and busyness. It was easy to forget that a time in God's presence might be far more valuable than one more task on the schedule.

On some days we were so preoccupied with problems to solve and organizations to run that we tended to depend upon our wit and perceived charm rather than the voice of the Spirit.

And, frankly, there were a few dark days when we were too low, too disappointed in ourselves, too confused to go where we should have been in the first place: bowed low at his feet.

But from the years come lessons, and we have learned to present our hearts to the Master. And from those experiences have come the thoughts on the pages of this book.

In writing *A Heart for the Master,* we went first to our

journals (the record of our spiritual journeys) and found comments we'd saved from men and women of previous generations who had a passion for truth, insight, and spiritual wholeness. Agree with everything each of them ever said or did? Hardly. But each of them did have something to teach us.

Then we matched those comments with appropriate Scriptures. Finally, we added an idea or two from our own experience. What has emerged from this effort is this book. The intent is to provide themes that will provoke both your soul and your mind. Think of each piece as an aid in getting your day pointed in the right direction.

May the peace of Christ be with you.

Gordon and Gail MacDonald
Canterbury, New Hampshire

~ 1 ~

He leads me beside still waters...

What do you think a typical day in the life of our Lord was like? Was he pressured? Stressed? Hassled by crowds, trapped in adversarial discussions with critics, inundated with the demands of the sick and disabled?

Take a second look. In fact, the Savior balanced his public life with private moments in the unfrequented places, and with simple, teachable, and broken people. He craved the quietness of the early morning hours, the solitude of the hills, and the stabilizing influence of intimate communion with the Father.

The spiritual masters, who tried to emulate Jesus, saw that noise, crowds, and hurriedness were serious obstacles to the work of growing in Christ's likeness. While they accepted the necessity of doing their work in such contexts, they regularly withdrew into the quieter places to hear the Father speak.

As our Master taught them, so they teach us. They counsel us to learn the rhythm of engagement and disengagement. Put another way: be at *work* in the world, then seek *rest* in God's presence. Our work, whatever it may be, is an offering to him when it is done with excellence; our *rest* becomes his gift to us, a time in which he enlarges the soul as a dwelling place for his Spirit.

❧

Is there a quiet stream underneath the fluctuating affirmation and rejections of my little world? Is there a still point where my life is anchored and from which I can reach out with hope and courage and confidence?

HENRI J.M. NOUWEN

The Lord is my shepherd, I shall not be in want.
He makes me lie down in green pastures,
he leads me beside quiet waters,
he restores my soul.
He guides me in paths of righteousness
for his name's sake.

PSALM 23:1-3

~ 2 ~

The Lord would speak to Moses face to face, as a man speaks with his friend.

Practical people—those who believe that things are accomplished through hard work—find it difficult to seek the Father's presence. Why be quiet when there is much to say? Why become still when there is much to do?

Ask Moses. Why would a man of his responsibilities disappear and commune with God? Why leave people waiting and projects unfinished to listen to Israel's God?

Simple. The burdens of leadership demanded more of Moses than his natural talents could provide. And people's incessant demands were a greater drain on Moses than his natural wisdom could support. To prevent exhaustion, he came regularly to this quiet place. And there he engaged with his Divine "Friend," where they talked as if face to face.

Each community needs people who understand that God desires a two-way conversation. He promises to hear everything about us, from the trivial to the profound. And he promises to speak into our hearts the wonderful words of life: of acceptance, of wisdom and guidance, of challenge, of assurance that all we are becoming and doing counts in his Kingdom.

❧

She is three months today, this first grandchild. I held her in my arms tonight and her mom let me give her the going-to-sleep bottle. As she sucked it to the last drop, she stared into my eyes.... As the time passed, it seemed as if the two of us, she and me, were one, attached by that union of undistracted eyes. Would that I could look at God so steadily.

FROM A GRANDFATHER'S JOURNAL

Now Moses used to take a tent and pitch it outside the camp some distance away, calling it the "tent of meeting." Anyone inquiring of the Lord would go to the tent of meeting outside the camp. And whenever Moses went out to the tent, all the people rose and stood at the entrances to their tents, watching Moses until he entered the tent. As Moses went into the tent, the pillar of cloud would come down and stay at the entrance, while the Lord spoke with Moses. Whenever the people saw the pillar of cloud standing at the entrance to the tent, they all stood and worshiped, each at the entrance to his tent. The Lord would speak to Moses face to face, as a man speaks with his friend.

EXODUS 33:7-11

~ 3 ~

Who are you, Lord?

A Christian conversion involves a call to follow Jesus Christ, to become like him in character and service. No one submits to this process easily. It is a lifelong struggle. Those who do not understand this will be continuously surprised and disappointed in themselves. Sooner or later, they will surrender the spiritual battle.

Wise and discerning is the person who acknowledges the hideous spirit of defiance within, a spirit that resists all Christ asks of us. He calls us to love our enemies; we prefer vengeance and retribution. He calls us to a humble, submissive life; we prefer self-assertiveness. He calls us to be teachable; we turn to our own ways.

Converting to Jesus and conforming ourselves to the new creation he is forming in us will often seem like all-out inner war. Each morning we must awaken with two questions on our hearts: (1) What will be his call to me today? and (2) From what part of me will come renewed resistance?

God knows the answers, but do we?

❧

When Jesus Christ comes with his spiritual power upon the soul to conquer it for himself, he hath no quiet landing place. He can set foot upon no ground but what he must fight for.

JOHN OWEN

In Damascus there was a disciple named Ananias. The Lord called to him in a vision, "Ananias!"

"Yes, Lord," he answered.

The Lord told him, "Go to the house of Judas on Straight Street and ask for a man from Tarsus named Saul, for he is praying...."

"Lord," Ananias answered, "I have heard many reports about this man and all the harm he has done to your saints in Jerusalem. And he has come here with authority from the chief priests to arrest all who call on your name."

But the Lord said to Ananias, "Go! This man is my chosen instrument to carry my name before the Gentiles and their kings and before the people of Israel."

ACTS 9:10-11,13-15

~ 4 ~

For I know my transgressions, and my sin is always before me....

When we seek to understand doctrine, we grow in our knowledge of God. When we make an effort to serve sacrificially, we gain satisfaction in knowing that the kingdom is a bit larger or stronger. And when we withdraw into quiet contemplation, we may hear him whisper special assurances into the soul.

However, it is only when we open our hearts, speaking frankly and even sorrowfully to God, naming our sins and acknowledging our sinfulness, that we are likely to gain humility. The Bible says of people who did this in ancient times, "they were cut to the heart." These were the people destined to grow in his Spirit.

The heart opened in such a way becomes purified. Impurities are washed away; the freshness of the Spirit invades. Weakness is replaced by new resolve and power.

❧

He who knows his sins is much greater than he who makes someone rise from the dead. He who can really cry for one hour about himself is greater than he who teaches the whole world; he who knows his own weakness is greater than he who sees the angels.

ISAAC OF NINEVEH

Have mercy on me, O God,
  according to your unfailing love;
according to your great compassion
  blot out my transgressions.
Wash away all my iniquiy
  and cleanse me from my sin.

Cleanse me with hyssop, and I will be clean;
  wash me, and I will be whiter than snow.
Let me hear joy and gladness;
  let the bones you have crushed rejoice.
Hide your face from my sins
  and blot out all my iniquity.

Create in me a pure heart, O God,
  and renew a steadfast spirit within me.
Do not cast me from your presence
  or take your Holy Spirit from me.
Restore to me the joy of your salvation
  and grant me a willing spirit, to sustain me.

PSALM 51:1-2, 7-12

~ 5~

What do you want me to do for you?

They were on their way to Jerusalem. It may have been that someone in the group had constructed a tight schedule, and had determined the time they should reach certain points along the way. What they would do hour by hour in Jerusalem during the holy days may have already been planned, what meetings and at what times. But of course that is the suspicion of a modern westerner.

Nevertheless, it's clear that Jesus and his disciples were in some kind of a hurry when the poor man crying out in the ditch was rudely told to be quiet.

But the ears of our Lord must have been acutely sensitive to the cries of people in ditches. Jesus stopped, and whatever schedule there might have been was immediately put on hold. Minutes later a blind beggar, a man who had been a nuisance to crowds for far too long, was made whole.

"When the people saw it, they praised God." Think of what they might have missed if our Lord had stuck to the schedule. And then think of the things we miss when we keep our eyes on our to-do lists and fail to respond to the needs of those we find in the ditch.

৽

[Francis] honored all men; that is, he not only loved but respected them all. What gave him extraordinary personal power was this: that from the pope to the beggar, from the sultan of Syria in his pavilion to the ragged robbers crawling out of the wood, there was never a man who looked into those brown burning eyes without being certain that Francis Bernadone was really interested in him ... [Francis] treated the whole mob of men as a mob of kings.

G.K. CHESTERTON ON FRANCIS OF ASSISI

As Jesus approached Jericho, a blind man was sitting by the road-side begging.... He called out, "Jesus, Son of David, have mercy on me!"

Those who led the way rebuked him and told him to be quiet, but he shouted all the more, "Son of David, have mercy on me!"

Jesus stopped and ordered the man to be brought to him. When he came near, Jesus asked him, "What do you want me to do for you?"

"Lord, I want to see," he replied.

Jesus said to him, "Receive your sight; your faith has healed you." Immediately he received his sight and followed Jesus, praising God. When all the people saw it, they also praised God.

LUKE 18:35, 38-43

~ 6 ~

I press on...

If a runner competes in a marathon (twenty-six miles), but is able to sprint ahead of the others only for the first hundred meters of the race, what do we expect the outcome will be? And what happens to the runner who leaves the prescribed course in search of a short cut? Or the athlete who is distracted by the applause of the crowd—or by fatigue or injury?

Storybooks are full of men and women who sprang from the starting line, intending to be "winners" for Christ, who were not to be found at the finish line.

Each day will bring novel enticements to God's "racer": to quit, or at least to slacken the pace. Such temptations must be met with a determined "no." "Looking unto Jesus ..." we fix our eyes once again straight ahead. Whatever the opinion of the spectators, whatever the difficulty of the course, whatever the temptation, we press on with the company of the saints.

This determination is honored by our Father. Those who renew their declaration—"this one thing I do..."—do not go unnoticed in heaven. The power to persevere is given to them.

❧

He taught me ... that the man who will keep right to the end of the chapter is the man whose gaze is fixed on God, whose joy is in God's company and whose heart is pure in its devotion to the will of God.

GEORGE YOUNG OF HIS MENTOR,
MISSIONARY GEORGE HUNTER

Brothers, I do not consider myself yet to have taken hold of it. But one thing I do: Forgetting what is behind and straining toward what is ahead, I press on toward the goal to win the prize for which God has called me heavenward in Christ Jesus.

All of us who are mature should take such a view of things. And if on some point you think differently, that too God will make clear to you. Only let us live up to what we have already attained.

PHILIPPIANS 3:13-16

~ 7 ~

Pure religion is...

The Christian faith was born into a world that regards the weak with contempt. Compassion, generosity, love: these were not the virtues prized by those who ran things, who had the power and the connections to make their will and their interests prevail.

Enter Jesus Christ. Stories began to circulate about one who engaged with lepers, the disabled, the outcasts, the children. Jesus would have been excused if, like almost all others, he had ignored them and sought the company of more important people. Instead he reached out to the lowly and the powerless.

Even friends could not understand this pattern. They tried to get him to allocate more of his time to people who had the "clout" to advance his interests. But what was Jesus' response? "They who ... [do not perceive themselves to be] sick have no need of a physician."

But before long, the hearts of the disciples began to change, and they began to see things as Jesus did. In Acts 3, on their way to the temple Peter and John spotted a beggar, prayed healing power into him, and pulled him to his feet. They came to understand this "pure religion" of their Master. The main resource of the weak, Jesus most treasured "audience," was his power revealed through love and service.

❧

The greatest pleasure I know is to do a good action by stealth and have it found out by accident.

CHARLES LAMB

Religion that God our Father accepts as pure and faultless is this: to look after orphans and widows in their distress and to keep oneself from being polluted by the world.

JAMES 1:27

~ 8 ~

Not everyone who says to me, "Lord, Lord," will enter the kingdom of heaven...

Today's culture finds virtually nothing attractive about the notion of obedience. This is the day of the *individual* who focuses on what's best for *me*, who praises the defiance of authority, and whose anthem is, in the words of the famous singer, "I did it my way."

Does this way of thinking ever seep into the Christian perspective? Is there a Christian individualism which appears saintly, but which is really fraudulent? "Not everyone who says ... Lord, Lord ... will enter." This sober warning from the past calls one to an inspection of the heart.

Jesus was not impressed with those who presented him with a menu of things done "in [his] name." He immediately discerned the hidden message: What we have done for you, we have done at our convenience and for our own advantage.

"Only he who does the will of my Father who is in heaven," is our Lord's requirement for Kingdom-citizenship. Thus, the Christ-follower includes *submission, servanthood,* and *humility* in the vocabulary of the heart. We learn to pray that we might learn to live at his bidding, for his purposes, in his time.

ॐ

The life that intends to be wholly obedient, wholly submissive, wholly listening, is astonishing in its completeness. Its joys are ravishing, its peace profound, its humility the deepest, its power world-shaking, its love enveloping, its simplicity that of a trusting child. It is the life and power in which the prophets and apostles lived. It is the life and power of Jesus of Nazareth, who knew that "when thine eye is single, thy whole body is full of light" (see Mt 6:22).

THOMAS KELLEY

"Not everyone who says to me, 'Lord, Lord,' will enter the kingdom of heaven, but only he who does the will of my Father who is in heaven. Many will say to me on that day, 'Lord, Lord, did we not prophesy in your name, and in your name drive out demons and perform many miracles?' Then I will tell them plainly, 'I never knew you. Away from me, you evildoers!'"

MATTHEW 7:21-23

~ 9 ~

These commandments that I give you today are to be upon your hearts...

Unless the word of God penetrates to the bottom of our hearts and thrives there, we are likely to live by a code of behavior that is easily exchanged for another when times change or when it becomes convenient.

The great secret of the Hebrews was a rule of life handed down by an everlasting God that was meant to reach deep into the heart. This rule involved more than a simple set of laws that could be endlessly debated in a search for loopholes. This rule, first written on tablets of stone, was also written in the human heart and transmitted from generation to generation. Godly people such as Joshua, Hannah, Samuel, David, Isaiah, and Esther took this rule to heart, and from their influence sprang up a community of the faithful. These people of integrity were always a minority, of course, but strong enough in numbers that their influence affected and elevated the nation.

What thrives in my heart? is a burning question of self-examination we should be asking ourselves on a daily basis. Our hearts were meant to be the library of life wherein his word of life might be stored so that its informing influence might be behind every thought, every choice, every word.

The central problem is that we do not know how to think, how to pray, how to cry, how to resist the deceptions of too many persuaders. There is no community of those who worry about integrity.

ABRAHAM JOSHUA HESCHEL

Hear, O Israel: The Lord our God, the Lord is one. Love the Lord your God with all your heart and with all your soul and with all your strength. These commandments that I give you today are to be upon your hearts. Impress them on your children. Talk about them when you sit at home and when you walk along the road, when you lie down and when you get up. Tie them as symbols on your hands and bind them on your foreheads. Write them on the doorframes of your houses and on your gates.

DEUTERONOMY 6:4-9

~ 10 ~

He built an altar there to the Lord.

The Lord's people have always known that any place—*any place!*—can be made into a sanctuary simply by calling on God's name. A hospital room, an office, a seat on a plane, a bedroom, a campsite. But a prison cell?

Here are two men stripped and beaten, shackled, and thrown into the inner cell where there is no fresh air, no light, no food, and no human contact beyond themselves. What a place to complain, to curse their luck, to vent rage or enter into a deep depression. Or ... what a place to worship. Which is what they did.

From out of the dark came a divine noise: the voices of two men "praying and singing hymns to God ... *and the other prisoners were listening to them."*

Two thoughts here.

First, if a dungeon can become a sanctuary, then any place can be made holy. And God will hear what is both said and sung to him.

Second, never be surprised at who might be listening when someone turns to worship. Prisoners, a jailer: all, apparently, who quickly showed themselves responsive. They knew genuineness when they heard it.

And where will you worship today?

৽৽

Are you building sacred palaces for yourself? I meant to write "places" to be sure, but I think I shall leave the word "palaces" for that is what any house becomes when it is sacred. The most important discovery of my whole life is that one can take a little rough cabin and transform it into a palace just by flooding it with thoughts of God.

FRANK LAUBACH

After they had been severely flogged, they were thrown into prison, and the jailer was commanded them to guard them carefully. Upon receiving such orders, he put them in the inner cell and fastened their feet in the stocks.

About midnight Paul and Silas were praying and singing hymns to God, and the other prisoners were listening to them. Suddenly there was such a violent earthquake that the foundations of the prison were shaken. At once all the prison doors flew open, and everybody's chains came loose. The jailer woke up, and when he saw the prison doors open, he drew his sword and was about to kill himself because he thought the prisoners had escaped. But Paul shouted, "Don't harm yourself! We are all here!"

The jailer called for lights, rushed in and fell trembling before Paul and Silas. He then brought them out and asked, "Sirs, what must I do to be saved?"

ACTS 16:23-30

~ 11 ~

She has been a great help to many people, including me.

As we read Scripture, we might be tempted to pass by portions such as Romans 16, where substance seems replaced by trivia. What does a list of names from an ancient generation have to do with a day so jammed with moral and ethical challenges?

But we ignore such passages to our peril. For here are a bevy of real, down-to-earth saints. Like us, they fought to survive. They were single and married, old and young, wealthy and impoverished. Together these people give us a wonderfully diverse picture of what the body of Christ, then and now, is supposed to look like. And they offer us snippets of Christ-like character.

There is Phoebe, a servant of the church. And Priscilla and Aquila, who risked their lives for a brother. Mary, who is known as a hard worker. How about Andronicus and Junias, outstanding among the apostles. Apelles, tested and approved. The mother of Rufus, who has been a mother to (Paul).

A line or two later, Paul writes, "Watch out for those who cause divisions [in the church].... Keep away from them" (Rom 16:17). His warning highlights the reason we should be drawn to the people mentioned earlier. If there are some to keep away from, then there are others to whom we should be drawn. Phoebe, Mary, Andronicus, Junias, Apelles, and Rufus' mother: these are our friends in Scripture. They give us hints of the kind of people we should be, and the kind of people we ought to seek out as friends for ourselves.

My calling and my friends, these are the two hinges on which my life turns.

FREDRICK SCHLIERMACHER

I commend to you our sister Phoebe, a servant of the church in Cenchrea. I ask you to receive her in the Lord in a way worthy of the saints and to give her any help she may need from you, for she has been a great help to many people, including me.

ROMANS 16:1-2

~ 12 ~

He must become greater;
I must become less.

We say of great athletes that they "went out at the top of their game." Meaning, he or she finished strong and would be missed by players and spectators alike.

What, then, can we say of John the Baptist? At the end of his public life, the crowds deserted him. Then he was arrested, and died a gruesome death in prison. Could this be described as going out at the top of one's game?

For John it was. His mission had been to identify the Christ and to see him ascend in the esteem of people as the Lamb of God. Jesus called him the greatest of prophets. Mission accomplished. John's success was never tied to public acclaim.

One of the great challenges of the Christian journey is to subordinate one's reputation to Christ's. How can we be known as faithful servants of the Lord if our service is predicated on being appreciated and applauded? For, as Scripture says, he will share his glory [the glory of his Father] with no one.

It is a constant matter of spiritual effort: to search our hearts in order to rid them of any tendency to "hold on," so that we are prepared when others turn from us to follow our Lord. For when they see Jesus—when they exalt him and, grow to be like him—we have been eminently successful. We are at the top of our "game."

❧

All I have cared about is the living presence of Christ; the life he lived, and the death he died, and the unique salvation he offers to a distracted world today.

MALCOLM MUGGERIDGE

An argument developed between some of John's disciples and a certain Jew over the matter of ceremonial washing. They came to John and said to him, "Rabbi, that man who was with you on the other side of the Jordan—the one you testified about—well, he is baptizing, and everyone is going to him."

To this John replied, "A man can receive only what is given him from heaven. You yourselves can testify that I said, 'I am not the Christ but am sent ahead of him.' The bride belongs to the bridegroom. The friend who attends the bridegroom waits and listens for him, and is full of joy when he hears the bridegroom's voice. That joy is mine, and it is now complete. He must become greater; I must become less."

JOHN 3:25-30

~ 13 ~

We will reap a harvest if we do not give up.

The farmer plants some crops before the winter snows, confident that spring will come and the plants will grow. He waits patiently for the warm sun and the spring rains. He fertilizes and, if necessary, irrigates. He never walks the fields impatiently. He knows that the harvest will come, and so he perseveres.

Perseverance is an outstanding mark of character in the Christian life as well. Cultivating a heart of wisdom is a lifelong process. The harvest of Christ-like fruitfulness may not come for years. We may be tempted, as Abraham was, to be impatient, to try to hurry God along. The temptations get worse when times get tough, when Heaven seems silent, when failures or adversities increase.

"If we do not give up ..." This is the description of the person who, day after day, practices the disciplines of the spirit, who pursues a life of loving actions, who makes the choices that are conditioned by a fidelity to Christ. As Christians, we know the day of vindication will come.

And then one day it does. The harvest is the result of many faithful choices, many faithful deeds. Few may have ever taken notice. But heaven has seen. And heaven rewards. The harvest is great.

❧

"He built fast boats which never finished."

FROM THE OBITUARY OF BOAT AND CAR RACER
MICKEY THOMPSON

Let us not become weary in doing good, for at the proper time we will reap a harvest if we do not give up. Therefore, as we have opportunity, let us do good to all people, especially to those who belong to the family of believers.

GALATIANS 6:9-10

~ 14 ~

Choose for yourself ... whom you will serve.

The Hebrews thrived on the stories of their past. In their storytelling, among the words most often used was *remember*. This powerful word meant more than simple recall. It called for a re–creation of a past event as if it were happening now, as if each person in each generation was a fresh part of it.

In such thinking, the sins of my fathers are my sins. The blessings given to my fathers are my blessings. What God has promised former generations, he has promised to us.

Another word the Hebrews often used was *choose*. It meant to renew one's decisions of the past. A choice made yesterday must be made again each day, a reaffirmation of what one believes and is committed to.

In our reading, Joshua, the commander of the tribes of Israel, remembers the story of God's call to Abraham, the miraculous deliverance out of Egypt, the various military victories during the wilderness journey, the gift of the Promised Land. "Now fear the Lord," cries Joshua. "Choose whom you will serve": embrace this all-gracious God who has led you so faithfully and renounce other gods who have no claim upon you.

๑๒

In everyman's career are certain points
Whereon he dares not be indifferent;
The world detects him clearly, if he dare,
As baffled at the game, and losing life.

ROBERT BROWNING

[And God said,] "Then you crossed the Jordan and came to Jericho. The citizens of Jericho fought against you, as did also the Amorites, Perizzites, Canaanites, Hittites, Girgashites, Hivites and Jebusites, but I gave them into your hands.... I gave you a land on which you did not toil and cities you did not build; and you live in them and eat from vineyards and olive groves that you did not plant.'

"Now fear the Lord and serve him with all faithfulness. Throw away the gods your forefathers worshiped beyond the River and in Egypt, and serve the Lord. But if serving the Lord seems undesirable to you, then choose for yourselves this day whom you will serve, whether the gods your forefathers served beyond the River, or the gods of the Amorites, in whose land you are living. But as for me and my household, we will serve the Lord."

JOSHUA 24:11, 13-15

~ *15* ~

...that you may declare the praises of him...

There are two dangers in reading these words. One is that we underestimate the significance of them and fail to understand that the genius of the Christian community is in its mission: to call people out of darkness into light. Our Lord would grieve if we were so silent.

A second danger is that we should act with arrogance and self-righteousness, speaking and acting as if we know everything and that others know nothing. Our Savior would never condone this.

How do we speak with the confidence of those who have been filled by his powerful Spirit, yet do so with voices that are respectful and humble? This question should not be far from our minds every time we engage the people about us. For as D.T. Niles once said, "We are all nothing more than beggars telling other beggars where we have found bread." We must hear this ancient challenge. Its call is fresh today. We too must remember what the God of Israel and Jesus Christ have done to gain our salvation. We too must choose each day whom we will serve. Yesterday's choice must be renewed, today and tomorrow and the day after that.

Never tire of choosing to serve him.

ॐ

There was never a world in greater need of men and women who know the way and can keep ahead and draw others to follow.

SAMUEL ZWEMER

But you are a chosen people, a royal priesthood, a holy nation, a people belonging to God, that you may declare the praises of him who called you out of darkness into his wonderful light. Once you were not a people, but now you are the people of God; once you had not received mercy, but now you have received mercy.

Dear friends, I urge you, as aliens and strangers in the world, to abstain from sinful desires, which war against your soul. Live such good lives among the pagans that, though they accuse you of doing wrong, they may see your good deeds and glorify God on the day he visits us.

1 PETER 2:9-12

~ 16 ~

If any man would come after me...

Deny yourself; take up your cross; follow me, Jesus said. Blunt words, those. Suffering and humiliation are prices one must be prepared to pay, if one chooses to walk in the way of our Lord.

We must refresh our choice to follow him daily—and perhaps several times each day—remembering that we are not guaranteed a life without tears, without pain. "A servant is not greater than his master," the Savior said. "They persecuted me; they will persecute you."

Many Christians prefer a faith that highlights success, popularity, and security, as if to say that if you give yourself to him, all that the larger world seeks will be yours also. You too will be prettier, happier, wealthier. We must not be motivated by such superficial offerings.

To love as Christ loves sometimes brings hurt. To hate sin as he hates it will sometimes bring rejection. To reach for the higher standards of character he modeled may invite ridicule. To offer oneself a sacrifice, as he did, could incur martyrdom.

But the way of the crucified and stripped Savior points to the throne of our Father.

❧

We follow a crucified and stripped Savior. These words go deep. They touch everything: motives, purposes, decisions, everything. Let them be with you as you prepare your spirit for the new life … you are coming to a battlefield. You cannot spend too much time with him alone.

AMY CARMICHAEL

Then he said to them all: "If anyone would come after me, he must deny himself and take up his cross daily and follow me. For whoever wants to save his life will lose it, but whoever loses his life for me will save it. What good is it for a man to gain the whole world, and yet lose or forfeit his very self?"

LUKE 9:23-25

~ 17 ~

...that all of them may be one.

Not long into our spiritual journey, each of us discovers certain inclinations—call them themes of behavior—in ourselves that, left unnamed and untreated, will leave us divided or fragmented in our inmost beings. Called to pursue oneness with our brothers and sisters in the Lord, we cannot obey because we are not, first of all, one within ourselves. It is best to face this difficult truth: there are territorial wars constantly in motion within each of us.

For some, this fragmentation exhibits itself as it did with Meyer's temptation, to jealousy toward one who seems, from a human perspective, to be better than himself. For others fragmentation emanates from an unreasonable desire for acceptance, or the need to be the center of attention. Perhaps it is generated when we are drawn to stretch the truth, resist authority, or exploit (possibly even use) people for our own convenience.

Personal honesty and repentance before God will arrest this process of fragmentation and return us to "oneness" or wholeness. Christ's prayer—that they may be one—is fulfilled, first, in the life of the person that prays that I may be one through the power of the cross. Then in renewed oneness of heart, we reach out to others of similar faith and attain the bondedness for which our Savior so earnestly prayed. The fellowship of the saints is the fellowship of repenting people.

&

It is related of the late F.B. Meyer that when he first went to the Northfield Conference, he attracted a crowd. People thronged to hear his special addresses. But, later, G. Campbell Morgan came to Northfield, and the people were lured by his brilliant Bible studies to desert Meyer. Meyer confessed a liability to jealously as he ministered to a smaller group. "The only way I can conquer my feelings," he said, "is to pray for him daily, which I do."

RALPH TURNBILL

"My prayer is not that you take them out of the world but that you protect them from the evil one. They are not of the world, even as I am not of it. Sanctify them by the truth; your word is truth. As you sent me into the world, I have sent them into the world. For them I sanctify myself, that they too may be truly sanctified."

JOHN 17:15-19

~ *18* ~

What is man that you are mindful of him...?

Creation itself is a great stage upon which the drama of reverence for God is often first played for the unbeliever. Something is seen in a discerning way that was never seen before. A sunset, a massive storm system, a celestial display. A newly born lamb, a fresh mountain stream, even a child's ear. And the heart is awakened to the grand designer behind it all who reminds us that he is very present to all things.

An astronomer once was asked if he ever contemplates a Creator in the galaxies he studies. "Oh, I made a choice a long time ago never to think about that," he responds. This is a limited mind, a closed heart at work.

The Christian looks at all things beautiful with two sets of eyes: The eyes of the mind, which ask, "What is the size, the shape, the origin of these things?" And the eyes of the heart, which ask, "What does this mean? And, what is the One who has made it trying to say? And, how shall I respond?"

❧

My eye came to rest on the delicate convolutions of [my new-born daughter's] ear—those intricate, perfect ears. The thought passed through my mind: "no, those ears were not created by any chance coming together of atoms in nature [the communist view]. They could have been created only by immense design." The thought was involuntary and unwanted. I crowded it out of my mind. But I never wholly forgot it or the occasion. I did not then know that, at that moment, the finger of God was first laid on my forehead.

WHITIKER CHAMBERS

When I consider your heavens,
the work of your fingers, the moon and the stars,
which you have set in place,
what is man that you are mindful of him,
the son of man that you care for him?
You made him a little lower than the heavenly beings
and crowned him with glory and honor....
O Lord, our Lord,
how majestic is your name in all the earth!

PSALM 8:3-5, 9

~ 19 ~

I will heal their waywardness and love them freely...

Nothing delights God more than wrapping his people in renewing grace. When Israel compounded its troubles with rebellion after rebellion, God remained close by, always waiting for the repentant prayer, the brokenness that cried out for a healing of the heart.

He called them to a land of beginning again, where people could "dwell again in his shade," where people might "flourish like the grain," where people might "blossom like the vine."

Why do we begin so many days preoccupied with trying to solve our problems on our own? Why do we ignore the tender call of the Lord who says, "Come to my presence and leave the shabby old coat at the door. You need never put it on again once I have clothed you in my kindness and grace."

There is a land of beginning again. It is called the place of forgiveness. We must go there.

How I wish that there were some wonderful place
Called the land of beginning again,
Where all our mistakes and all our heartaches
And all our poor selfish grief
Could be dropped like a shabby old coat
at the door and never put on again.

ANONYMOUS, FROM THE WRITINGS OF
WILLIAM BARCLAY

"I will heal their waywardness
and love them freely,
for my anger has turned away from them.
I will be like the dew to Israel;
he will blossom like a lily.
Like a cedar of Lebanon
he will send down his roots."

HOSEA 14:4-5

~ 20 ~

Today you will be with me in paradise...

We must not be swept up and influenced by the habit of
those who seek retaliation and vengeance each time they are
offended or attacked. Our minds are quick to justify our
anger, our instinct to strike back, our need to be vindicated.

The conduct and composure of Christ on the cross must
be among the things we study most. For it is in his dying that
he offers us the most intense model of how the believer is to
live.

Jesus' attitude toward those who nailed him to the cross
was one of forgiveness. Toward those who jeered and
ridiculed him, he remained silent. Toward a dying criminal
at his side he extended himself graciously, inviting him to
join him in paradise. Three acts of dignity: forgiveness,
silence, and graciousness.

We must ask ourselves if these qualities of conduct exist in
our Christian character on a day to day basis. These are the
significant marks of one who follows him in life and in
death.

ঞ

...whether by nature or from grace I do not know, but I had rather be trampled upon than be the trampler. I could find it more agreeable to my own feelings to go and weep with the relatives of the men whom the English have killed than to rejoice at the laurels they have won.

HENRY MARTYN, WRITING AS A CIVILIAN PASSENGER
ABOARD A BRITISH WARSHIP AS IT SHELLED CAPETOWN

Two other men, both criminals, were also led out with him to be executed. When they came to the place called the Skull, there they crucified him, along with the criminals—one on his right, the other on his left. Jesus said, "Father, forgive them, for they do not know what they are doing." And they divided up his clothes by casting lots.

The people stood watching, and the rulers even sneered at him. They said, "He saved others; let him save himself if he is the Christ of God, the Chosen One."

One of the criminals who hung there hurled insults at him: "Aren't you the Christ? Save yourself and us!"

But the other criminal rebuked him. "Don't you fear God," he said, "since you are under the same sentence? We are punished justly, for we are getting what our deeds deserve. But this man has done nothing wrong."

Then he said, "Jesus, remember me when you come into your kingdom."

Jesus answered him, "I tell you the truth, today you will be with me in paradise."

LUKE 23:32-35, 39-43

~ 21 ~

Be filled with the Holy Spirit.

Could it be that we over-explore the world and "under-explore" the heart? In the former we think we shall find all the answers to the good and happy life. But in the latter we find that we are in strange territory.

The world is explored with things like computers, satellites, and measuring devices of all kinds. The heart is explored with the assistance of Scripture, prayer, spiritual listening, praise, and worship. Both efforts are honorable and right. To ignore one at the expense of the other is to be out of balance.

God does not ask us to surrender our capabilities and adventures in the outer world. But he does ask that we enter that world through the doorway of the heart. The place where we have heard him speak and give direction. Then we shall be ready today for the business that lies before us.

❧

Once upon a time, an ancient monastic tale says, the Elder said to the businessperson: "As the fish perishes on dry land, so you perish when you get entangled in the world. The fish must return to the water and you must return to the Spirit."

And the businessperson was aghast. "Are you saying that I must give up my business and go into a monastery?" the person asked.

And the Elder said, "Definitely not. I am telling you to hold on to your business and go into your heart."

JOAN CHITTISTER

Be very careful, then, how you live—not as unwise but as wise, making the most of every opportunity, because the days are evil. Therefore do not be foolish, but understand what the Lord's will is. Do not get drunk on wine, which leads to debauchery. Instead, be filled with the Spirit.

EPHESIANS 5:15-18

~ 22 ~

Everyone is asking for you.

It was the day after Sabbath. The previous day, the Lord had engaged people in the synagogue, healed the sick, answered questions, taught the crowds. Who would question his right to while away the next morning? Yet the Scripture says that very early in the morning, he went out into the hills to pray.

What is more important: a body in need of rest or a soul in need of revitalization? Power had gone out of Jesus; it had to be renewed. Busyness could conceivably provoke inner restlessness and confusion; Jesus knew he would profit from hearing a restatement of his mission and the approval of his Father. Friends and crowds would soon be coming at him, making demands upon his time. He would need courage and determination to stand his ground and do the right thing.

Imagine the Lord in the hills, alone, in communion with the Father, quiet. And then ask yourself what you need most of all.

❧

Remember a long life of steady, consistent holy labor will produce twice as much fruit as one shortened and destroyed by spasmodic and extravagant exertions. Be careful and sparing of your strength when or where exertion is unnecessary.... I speak with all tenderness, I tell you that I see ambition to be your chief mental besetment, not a besetment if rightly directed but if unsanctified, warped to an idol object.

CATHERINE BOOTH, 23,
TO HER HUSBAND, WILLIAM

The next morning he [Jesus] was up long before daybreak and went out alone into the wilderness to pray.

Later, Simon and the others went out to find him, and told him, "Everyone is asking for you."

But he replied, "We must go on to other towns as well, and give my message to them too, for that is why I came."

So he traveled throughout the province of Galilee, preaching in the synagogues and releasing many from the power of demons.

MARK 1:35-39, TLB

~ 23 ~

Endure hardship as discipline...

Read the life of any of God's champions, and you will inevitably find their suffering experiences. In such moments they acquired the depth and breadth of life that generates our admiration and makes us want to know them better.

No one in his or her right mind would wish to suffer. Who could possibly wish for the suffering of physical pain, betrayal, persecution, ostracism, poverty? Who would want this? No one!

But when suffering comes—and it comes to most of us— there is a choice we must make.

Some will choose to fight the suffering moment; they will cry out bitterly, blame others, go into denial or, as Job's wife encouraged him to do, curse God and wish for death.

But there are others who will resolve that, in the suffering, they will hear God speak. They will seize the moment for "growth of soul." The heart will become more tender; the mind will store up truths that cannot be heard under any other circumstances. Friends will become more dear; the Scripture will provide greater wisdom; and the company of the committed will become more real. And a "harvest of righteousness" will be the result. It is often in the context of suffering that saints are born.

❧

I walked a mile with Pleasure
She chattered all the way,
But left me none the wiser
For all she had to say.

I walked a mile with sorrow
And ne'er a word said she,
But, oh, the things I learned from her
When sorrow walked with me.

FROM BARCLAY ON MATTHEW

Endure hardship as discipline; God is treating you as sons. For what son is not disciplined by his father? If you are not disciplined (and everyone undergoes discipline), then you are illegitimate children and not true sons. Moreover, we have all had human fathers who disciplined us and we respected them for it. How much more should we submit to the Father of our spirits and live!

HEBREWS 12:7-9

~ *24* ~

The good shepherd lays down his life for the sheep...

God has given us powerful imaginations. As children we see ourselves as great athletes, dancers, or soldiers. In youth we dream of being the lover or the loved. And in adulthood we set the eyes of fantasy on career success, the applause that ascends to the leader, and the attention given to the so-called life of the party.

Why not sometimes see ourselves as the sheep whom Jesus seeks? Cold, weary, wounded, lost. The Savior leaves the relative comfort of the fire and the fold and comes to the wilderness in the night to find us. He lifts us from the place of entrapment, binds the wounds, provides the water to slake the thirst, and lifts us over his shoulder. And carries us home.

It is renewing and humbling to the soul to occasionally walk into the story Jesus has told and reenact the story of the lost sheep for whom the Good Shepherd risks his life. And when we do, our faith is freshened, and our love for him is rekindled.

I was a stricken deer
That left the herd long since.
With many an arrow deep in-fixed
my panting side was charged
When I withdrew to seek a tranquil death
in distant shades.

There was I found by one who
had himself
Been hurt by the archers.
In his side he bore
And in his hands and feet, the cruel scars.

With gentle force soliciting the darts
he drew them forth,
And healed and bade me live.

WILLIAM COWPER

*"I am the good shepherd; I know my sheep and my sheep know me—
just as the Father knows me and I know the Father—and I lay down
my life for the sheep.... The reason my Father loves me is that I lay
down my life—only to take it up again. No one takes it from me, but
I lay it down of my own accord. I have authority to lay it down and
authority to take it up again. This command I received from my
Father."*

JOHN 10:14-15, 17-18

~ 25 ~

This is my Son ... listen to him.

Simon Peter seemed to have had a poor sense of timing. He spoke too quickly. Here he was on the mountaintop, one of three privy to this most sacred of conversations between our Lord, Moses, and Elijah. The ambience, Scripture says, was one of "glorious splendor." We would like to think that, had we been there, our behavior would have been appropriate to the moment: reverential silence.

But surely some of us would have fallen into the way of Simon Peter. Like him, we would have reduced the remarkable moment to the confines of a program. "Master, this is wonderful! We'll put up three shelters ..." Luke understates the situation when he comments on Peter's remark: this bumbling apostle spoke, "not even knowing what he was saying."

Heaven's message is instructive: This is my son ... listen to him. It was time for Peter to relinquish his need to control, to give his opinion. It was time, heaven was saying, for Peter to be still and strain to hear every word that the Master might say.

❦

How do you know whether a man is a Christian? The answer is that his mouth is shut. I like this forthrightness of the Gospel. People need to have their mouths shut, "stopped." They are forever talking about God, and criticizing God, and pontificating about what God should or should not do, and asking, "why does God allow this or that?" You do not begin to be a Christian until your mouth is shut, is stopped, and you are speechless and have nothing to say.

MARTYN LLOYD-JONES

Eight days later he took Peter, James, and John with him into the hills to pray. And as he was praying, his face began to shine, and his clothes became dazzling white and blazed with light. Then two men appeared and began talking with him—Moses and Elijah! They were splendid in appearance, glorious to see; and they were speaking of his death at Jerusalem, to be carried out in accordance with God's plan.

Peter and the others had been very drowsy and had fallen asleep. Now they woke up and saw Jesus covered with brightness and glory, and the two men standing with him. As Moses and Elijah were starting to leave, Peter, all confused and not even knowing what he was saying, blurted out, "Master, this is wonderful! We'll put up three shelters—one for you and one for Moses and one for Elijah!"

But even as he was saying this, a bright cloud formed above them; and terror gripped them as it covered them. And a voice from the cloud said, "This is my Son, my Chosen One; listen to him."

LUKE 9:28-35, TLB

~ *26* ~

We ought to lay down our lives for our brothers.

There are two experiences in human behavior most likely to produce stories of ultimate heroism, the kind where people die for one another. The first is when a mother endangers herself to protect her children. The second example is a soldier who sacrifices himself for his buddies on the battlefield.

"Very rarely will anyone die for a righteous man ..." St. Paul wrote, taking note of the fact that we are normally committed to self-preservation rather than ultimate heroism.

When Jesus called his followers to love one another, he had the standard of ultimate heroism in mind. "Love one another," he said, "as I have loved you." We know how he demonstrated his love. And John has this in mind when he writes, "we ought to lay down our lives for our brothers."

The necessity may never arise for most of us to actually die for one another. But such ultimate heroism should mark the way I speak of you and to you, how I am prepared to care for you, what I am prepared to give to you, and the extent to which I will support you in your moment of need.

❦

"I would gladly have taken that bullet."
IN A NOTE FROM JIMMY STEWART TO RONALD REAGAN,
RECOVERING FROM AN ASSASSINATION ATTEMPT

This is how we know what love is: Jesus Christ laid down his life for us. And we ought to lay down our lives for our brothers. If anyone has material possessions and sees his brother in need but has no pity on him, how can the love of God be in him? Dear children, let us not love with words or tongue but with actions and in truth.

1 JOHN 3:16-18

~ 27 ~

We are being renewed every day...

Paul never feared growing old. The aches and pains, the physical signs of aging, the accumulation of fatigue—all signs of the loss of youth—never seemed to bother him. For Paul, the issue had much more to do with the heart, the interior space.

Daily renewal for Paul was a heart-matter. His priotities: a growing personal vision of Kingdom possibilities, knowing Christ better, developing people in Christlikeness, acquiring a contentment of spirit that was not controlled by circumstances. The more his body aged, the more his heart matured.

Like the apostle Paul, we make daily choices: Is it more important to be young on the surface, or youthful in the heart? It is difficult to give them equal priority.

For Paul, the choice was simple and obvious. The outer man would go the way of his fathers: toward the dust of death. But the inner man would reach out for Christ every day and grow more powerful with the years. It comes as no surprise then when, at the end of his life, Paul is still declaring, "that I may know him ..."

We know a lot of older people whose lives end in unpleasantness. And then we know a few whose lives end with a flare of vitality and tenderness. A generalization perhaps: but it is usually clear that the former have hated their aging and tried to maintain the fiction of youth. But the latter have moved toward Christ day by day, and in their inner space, they have remained forever young.

❧

In the factory we make cosmetics; in the store we sell hope.

CHARLES REVLON

Therefore we do not lose heart. Though outwardly we are wasting away, yet inwardly we are being renewed day by day.

2 CORINTHIANS 4:16

~ 28 ~

For the Lord gives wisdom...

It is tempting to believe that the most successful person is the one who talks more, does more, and owns more. We are easily intrigued by those who visit far-off places, drop famous names, and attract frequent applause. From a distance, such people give every indication that they possess the secrets of life. The close-up view, however, may reveal another story.

The Scriptures do not exalt the successful person. Rather, they honor the wise person. The one who understands life's direction. The one who walks with a confidence grounded in eternal truth. The one who discerns the meaning of things and events. The one whose words bring peace, understanding, empowerment.

While the Scriptures are not hostile to success, the writers of holy truth appreciated the fact that genuinely wise people may not always be successful, at least by society's standards. And successful people may not always be wise, at least by God's standards.

Better to set wisdom among our highest pursuits. And if success—the more obvious kind—follows, we shall know that it was a result of God's gracious purpose for us.

A life all turbulence and noise
May seem to him that leads it
wise and to be praised.
But wisdom is a pearl with most success,
Sought in still waters.

WILLIAM COWPER

My son, if you accept my words and store up my commands within you, turning your ear to wisdom and applying your heart to understanding, and if you call out for insight and cry aloud for understanding, and if you look for it as for silver and search for it as for hidden treasure, then you will understand the fear of the Lord and find the knowledge of God.

PROVERBS 2:1-5

~ 29 ~

God heard his prayers because of his strong desire to obey...

We can do just about anything in the world of Christian faith without deep spiritual power. With sufficient talent, practice, and, when necessary, the cooperation of others, it is possible to project the appearance of a saint. In fact, some good might even be accomplished ... at least in the short range.

But it is in the ministry of intercession—that passionate effort in which we lift people and situations to God—that real sainthood is developed. Intercession is most often done in private or in the company of a few. It does not attract applause; it rarely exerts immediate influence; it does not pay well.

But spirited intercession changes situations and people. And it will change us, if no one else. We see people (our enemies and friends both) in a new light. We gain a new kind of optimism that all things will work together in alignment with his purposes. We gain control over our fears, our doubts, and our angers. Upon our knees, we find ourselves in possession of a new vision of God.

෯෫

There are many kinds of service that make no demand upon spirituality for their success. Preaching may be an art in which there is no power of the spirit.... Social service may make a fair show in the official returns without any glow of spirit mindedness. Church music may be the kind that does not call for the travail and anguish of intercession. The man of prayer must be a man of God.

SAMUEL CHADWICK

Yet while Christ was here on earth he pleaded with God, praying with tears and agony of soul to the only one who would save him from [premature] death. And God heard his prayers because of his strong desire to obey God at all times.

And even though Jesus was God's Son, he had to learn from experience what it was like to obey, when obeying meant suffering. It was after he had proved himself perfect in this experience that Jesus became the Giver of eternal salvation to all those who obey him. For remember that God has chosen him to be a High Priest with the same rank as Melchizedek.

HEBREWS 5:7-10, TLB

~ 30 ~

I am among you as one who serves...

Our Lord never tried to impress anyone. He wore the clothes of the poor, did the work of a common man, made friends with the lowly, and told stories a child would understand. He refused the games of power, wealth, and intellectual arrogance. He could have awed people with what he knew about Heaven, with spectacular magic shows, and with displays of glitzy majesty. Indeed, people would have been attracted by such things. But that was not his way.

There was no insincerity in Jesus. No manipulation, no effort to intimidate or impress. What you saw was what you got. The Son of God in the form of a man, in the role of a servant. And from that position of weakness, he changed the world.

We need to ask ourselves why we have this driving need to be something that we're not. For if this is our way, then we are impressing everyone else, but certainly not the one who said, "I am among you as one who serves."

The cross, the ultimate symbol of servanthood, releases us to be who we actually are: men and women touched by his love, filled by his power, approved by him, called to be servants.

❦

I find I am shedding hypocrisy in human relationships. What a rest that will be! The most exhausting thing in life, I have discovered, is being insincere. That is why so much of social life is exhausting; one is wearing a mask. I have shed my mask.

ANN MORROW LINDBERG

While he [Jesus] was still speaking a crowd came up, and the man who was called Judas, one of the Twelve, was leading them. He approached Jesus to kiss him, but Jesus asked him, "Judas, are you betraying the Son of Man with a kiss?"

When Jesus' followers saw what was going to happen, they said, "Lord, should we strike with our swords?" And one of them struck the servant of the high priest, cutting off his right ear.

LUKE 22:47-50

~ 31 ~

...prepared to do any good work.

We are told that in the high places of the great cathedrals, there are nooks and crannies where sculptors carved statuary that no one but God could easily see. It was the artist's way of saying, "What I have done, I have done for God. And I would do it just as excellently if no one else in the world ever knew that it was there."

The Christ-follower should never be at peace with habitual laziness, mediocrity, or leaving things uncompleted. While none of us can be expert in everything, we should never give God or his people something less than the best we can do.

Are we ever tempted to think that God doesn't care about the quality of our worship, our service, our character? Has our view of God become so warped that we begin to think of him as a benevolent old man who is grateful for any "crumb" of attention we throw his way? If any of this is so, we need a revival in our theology, our perception of the nature of God.

A revival might start with a reminder that Almighty God has never given us anything but his best. Creation is his handiwork, Jesus is his Son, the Holy Spirit is the expression of his unbounded power, and Scripture is his magnificent "letter" to us. Can anyone find shabbiness here?

Each day we should consider resharpening our standard of excellence. His best calls for our best from the tiniest detail to the most significant of efforts.

৯৩

We are what we repeatedly do. Excellence, then, is not an
act, but a habit.

ARISTOTLE

In a large house there are articles not only of gold and silver, but also
of wood and clay; some are for noble purposes and some for ignoble.
If a man cleanses himself from the latter, he will be an instrument for
noble purposes, made holy, useful to the Master and prepared to do
any good work.

2 TIMOTHY 2:20-21

~ 32 ~

And the peace of God ... will guard your hearts and your minds...

Left uncontrolled, the heart appears to drift downwards in its preoccupations. It seems to prefer to dwell on resentments and angers, envies and jealousies, issues that center on self-aggrandizement and self-preservation and away from the interests of God and the interests of others. It inclines toward the banal, the trivial, the exploitative. It is a harsh conclusion to which he comes, but we just might have to acknowledge that, St. Paul was right when he wrote, "I know that nothing good lives in me, that is, in my sinful nature."

Scripture calls for the Christ-follower to cultivate a disciplined mind. Writing to the Philippians, for example, Paul offered a menu of qualities that ought to mark the Christian mind: thoughts which are true, noble, right, pure, lovely, admirable, excellent, and praiseworthy. "Think about such things," he encouraged.

How to do this in a world in which the primary pursuit is pleasure and profit, which seems to revel in attracting the mind toward base things? Perhaps this is one of the major themes of the Sabbath pause: to pray, asking God's Spirit to fix our minds upon the higher things, the things of Christ, the noble matters which raise a person to the levels of humanity that God intended when he created us.

You cannot play with the animal in you without becoming wholly animal, play with falsehood without forfeiting your right to truth, play with cruelty without losing your sensitivity of mind. He who wants to keep his garden tidy doesn't reserve a plot for weeds.

DAG HAMMARSKJÖLD

Rejoice in the Lord always. I will say it again: Rejoice! Let your gentleness be evident to all. The Lord is near. Do not be anxious about anything, but in everything, by prayer and petition, with thanksgiving, present your requests to God. And the peace of God, which transcends all understanding, will guard your hearts and your minds in Christ Jesus.

PHILIPPIANS 4:4-7

~ 33 ~

Though you have not seen him, you love him.

We might want to take comfort in the story of Simon Peter, the impulsive disciple. He has important things to teach us— most of us, anyway. He seems quick with his words, clumsy in action, slow in growth. One wonders, at first, why our Lord would wish to have a man like this so close to him.

It is Peter who tries to dissuade Jesus from talking of future suffering, who grows cocky and almost drowns while walking toward Jesus on the water, who totally loses his nerve when challenged to acknowledge his association with Jesus in the home of the high priest. After a while, you start to cringe every time Peter is said to open his mouth or spring into action. What will he do next?

Had we walked in Peter's sandals, we might have been tempted to back off before Jesus could ask us to withdraw. But he didn't quit, and Jesus didn't ask him to. Instead, he appears to have turned every blunder into an eventual growth experience. Having made his mistakes and having discovered his flaws, he always pushed ahead to maturity. To put it in his own words: "These have come so that your faith, of greater worth than gold,... may be proved genuine and may result in praise, glory and honor when Jesus Christ is revealed."

Better Peter's initial bunglings and recoveries than our superficial conservativism, which takes no chances and eventuates in no blessings.

❧

Peter, had I
   followed him as eagerly
   served him as loyally
   loved him as utterly
   agreed to die with him as willingly
as you,
And then denied him as dastardly,
   thrice,
I too would weep when roosters crow.
But
because I have done all things
conservatively
and faced death not at all,
   I have neither wept
   nor been tenderly restored
   and called a rock.

OOSTERVEEN

*In this you greatly rejoice, though now for a little while you may have
had to suffer grief in all kinds of trials. These have come so that your
faith—of greater worth than gold, which perishes even though
refined by fire—may be proved genuine and may result in praise,
glory and honor when Jesus Christ is revealed.*

1 PETER 1:6-7

~ 34 ~

You are the salt of the earth...
you are the light of the world.

In how many human transactions will we be engaged before
the end of this day? Specific conversations with those we love
most and those we know as friends. Encounters with those in
our lives of work: colleagues, venders, and customers. To this
list add meetings with strangers, connections through the
phone and e-mail, and random exchanges at the market,
even in traffic.

Assume that in every one of these appointments—even
those that seem most insignificant—we can offer either a posi-
tive or negative influence upon another person. By a loving or
affirming word we can build a greater element of value in
another. In an act of servanthood we can make another person's world a calmer, steadier place. In a gesture of deference,
we can obey the Lord when he said, "hold others to a higher
honor than yourself." In a moment of generosity, we can ele-
vate another to a level they might not otherwise have reached.

But also remember that we can do just the opposite. In our
many transactions we are capable of diminishing our brother
or sister by a scornful word, corrupting another person's
world by an act of selfishness, and devaluing another person
through intimidation.

God has given us this strange and awesome influential
power: to build in one another's lives or to harm one another.
Which will it be? The power Christ gives makes it possible for
us to do the first.

෧෨

A dying old man once made a startling confession. "One day when I was young, I was playing with some other boys at a crossroads. We reversed a signpost so that its arms were pointing in the wrong direction, and I've never ceased wondering how many people were sent in the wrong direction by what we did."

FROM THE NOTES OF
WILLIAM BARCLAY

"You are the salt of the earth; but if salt has lost its taste, how shall its saltness be restored? It is no longer good for anything except to be thrown out and trodden under foot by men.

"You are the light of the world. A city set on a hill cannot be hid. Nor do men light a lamp and put it under a bushel, but on a stand, and it gives light to all in the house. Let your light so shine before men, that they may see your good works and give glory to your Father who is in heaven."

MATTHEW 5:13-16, RSV

~ 35 ~

Lord, lay not this sin to their charge...

Stephen's dying words were saturated with grace. They could have been full of protest or anger. They could have been expressions of pain and self-pity. But they were words of forgiveness and reflected similar words on the lips of Christ at the cross.

Could it be that when a person speaks in the final moment of life, that person is revealing to us the core of the soul? Could we be hearing the most profound of truths they have experienced in life, as they have embraced and lived it? "For they breathe truth that breathe their words in pain."

We know from the narrator of this story that a youngish man, Saul of Tarsus, stood near the place where Stephen was dying. And we presume that he heard Stephen's words. And it is quite reasonable to believe that Stephen's prayer burned its way down into his soul. From the heart of Stephen to the heart of Saul of Tarsus: a word of grace rather than a curse.

And the word did not lose its force. Rather—as words of grace are wont to do—it grew, surged, overwhelmed his inner life. Until one day on the road to Damascus he heard other words: Saul, why do you persecute me? And the word of forgiving grace from Stephen was followed up by the word of saving grace from the resurrected Jesus.

We never know when words we speak in the extreme moment—in dying, in suffering, in a time of failure or betrayal, in great duress—will be heard by someone else and become the initial pointers through which they find their way to heaven.

❦

The tongues of dying men
    Enforce attention, like deep harmony:
When words are scarce
    They're seldom spent in vain;
For they breathe truth that
    breathe their words in pain.

SHAKESPEARE
FROM KING RICHARD II

While they were stoning him, Stephen prayed, "Lord Jesus, receive my spirit." Then he fell on his knees and cried out, "Lord, do not hold this sin against them." When he had said this, he fell asleep.

ACTS 7:59-60

~ 36 ~

Can you drink the cup that I am going to drink?

To sit at the right or the left hand of the Lord of the universe. This is not imagery that immediately grabs the imagination of someone from the twenty-first century. We have our own cultural imagery to describe the desire to have the best, to be the most privileged. But the sons of Zebedee (and their mother) are not alone in their wish for recognition. It's in us as well.

Can you drink the cup that I am going to drink? Unlike these men, we know that the cup of which Jesus spoke was the cross. It is as if he had said, "The seats you desire are just beyond Calvary. Do you care to walk in that direction with me?"

Who will be the honored ones when we stand in his presence? Those who worked the hardest or who achieved the greatest notoriety? Those most generous with their money or most faithful to the program of the church? Or those who suffered as a result of their faithfulness to the Savior?

"Whoever wants to become great among you must be your servant ... your slave." Most of us are raised with the aspiration to be kings, to live a trouble-free existence. He asks us to embrace the opposite: servanthood and a willingness to suffer. Our day ahead must be planned with this in mind. For that is where honor in the Kingdom is found.

❧

Wanted: young, skinny, wiry fellows not over eighteen. Must be expert riders, willing to risk death daily. Orphans preferred.

NINETEENTH CENTURY CLASSIFIED AD
FOR PONY EXPRESS RIDERS

Then the mother of Zebedee's sons came to Jesus with her sons and, kneeling down, asked a favor of him.

"What is it you want?" he asked.

She said, "Grant that one of these two sons of mine may sit at your right and the other at your left in your kingdom."

"You don't know what you are asking," Jesus said to them. "Can you drink the cup I am going to drink?"

"We can," they answered.

Jesus said to them, "You will indeed drink from my cup, but to sit at my right or left is not for me to grant. These places belong to those for whom they have been prepared by my Father."

MATTHEW 20:20-23

~ 37 ~

But now, Lord, what do I look for?
My hope is in you.

Our modern age of communications has provided for us amazing vehicles for conveying information: first the telegraph, then the telephone, the radio, the television, and now the Internet. Of course having the capability to communicate is no guarantee that we have something of substance to communicate.

When he was first told that the telegraph would make it possible for the people of Maine to speak instantly to the people of Texas, Thoreau asked, "But what if the people of Maine have nothing to say to the people of Texas?"

What if we should discover that, having acquired our cellular phones, our e-mail addresses, our sound equipment, and television programs, we have nothing of value to say? That we are experts in communicating nothing?

It profits us as Christ-followers to listen carefully to ourselves. Even in our most serious moments: what are we saying? Do we speak to one another thoughtfully, respectfully, spiritually? Would anyone know by our conversation that we have been with Christ and bear his imprint upon us?

The spiritual masters often took vows of silence for this very purpose. They saw no use in saying anything until they had first listened. Some chose not to speak for years. If their efforts were a bit excessive, their intentions were good. At least they point us in a worthy direction: the place of quietness where we finally become still enough to let the words of heaven seep into our souls. Then it might be time to speak.

❧

If our life is poured out in useless words we will never hear anything in the depths of our hearts, where Christ lives and speaks in silence. We will never be anything, and in the end, when the time comes for us to declare who and what we are, we shall be found speechless at the moment of the crucial decision: for we shall have said everything and exhausted ourselves in speech before we had anything to say.

THOMAS MERTON

My heart grew hot within me,
and as I meditated, the fire burned; then I spoke with my tongue:
"Show me, O Lord, my life's end
and the number of my days;
let me know how fleeting is my life."

PSALM 39:3-4

~ 38 ~

...that they may be one...

When followers of Christ come to the Lord's table and eat the bread and drink the wine together, they believe that they celebrate the presence of Christ. Jesus goes a step further when he says that whenever two or more come together and acknowledge his name as their point of connection, he is there. In other words, when believers are present to one another, a sacramental connection is in motion. Jesus is there.

This elevates Christian fellowship to the highest possible level. It challenges the believer to a consciousness of Christ's presence in every relationship. Knowing this, we guard our speech; we are careful to treat each other with respect; we are more diligent with our choice of activity; and we are more mindful of one another's needs.

This is what draws the people of a larger world in our direction. They are fascinated not as much by the Christ of our doctrine, but the Christ who pervades these relationships of ours.

❧

Christianity means community through Jesus Christ and in Jesus Christ. No Christian community is more or less than this. Whether it be a brief, single encounter or the daily fellowship of years, Christian community is only this. We belong to one another only through and in Jesus Christ. What does this mean? It means, first, that a Christian needs others because of Jesus Christ. It means, second, that a Christian comes to others only through Jesus Christ. It means, third, that in Jesus Christ we have been chosen from eternity, accepted in time, and united for eternity.

DIETRICH BONHOEFFER

"My prayer is not for them alone. I pray also for those who will believe in me through their message, that all of them may be one, Father, just as you are in me and I am in you. May they also be in us so that the world may believe that you have sent me. I have given them the glory that you gave me, that they may be one as we are one: I in them and you in me. May they be brought to complete unity to let the world know that you sent me and have loved them even as you have loved me."

JOHN 17:20-23

~ 39 ~

The Son of Man came to seek and to save what was lost...

In Jesus' time, tax collectors were considered to be among the most corrupt and exploitative of all people. It should not surprise us, then, that one of the ways the enemies of our Lord tried to tarnish his reputation was to point out that he occasionally engaged with these most despised of all people.

Take, for example, the time when Jesus journeyed toward Jerusalem to celebrate the holy days. Near Jericho, Zacchaeus, a tax collector, climbed into a tree overlooking the path Jesus was to take. His explanation? "He wanted to see Jesus." One suspects, however, that Zacchaeus had deeper intentions. A part of his heart, perhaps not even known to him, was troubled about life and yearned for a new beginning. He could claim that he was curious to see Christ; but one senses that he had a deeper urge to meet the Lord.

And Jesus seemed quite aware of this longing when he stopped at the place where Zacchaeus waited in the branches of the tree and called him down. Before long the two were engaged in conversation ... at the tax collector's house. That Jesus would talk with the man was one thing. But that Jesus would enter his home, was something else. This act of entering Zachaeus' home enraged both his critics and his friends.

Jesus later explained his actions. I've come to seek and save lost people, he said. Implication: you don't find lost people by shouting at them or demonizing them. You move in their direction, enter their homes and places of work, speak their language, and take them seriously. Most people in that time found this difficult, if not impossible, to do. But not our Lord. He went where the lost were to be found. And that is how he located us.

ஒ

The kingdom is to be in the midst of your enemies. And he who will not suffer this does not want to be of the kingdom of Christ; he wants to be among friends, to sit among the roses and the lilies, not with the bad people but the devout people. O you blasphemers and betrayers of Christ. If Christ had done what you are doing, who would have ever been spared?

MARTIN LUTHER

As Jesus was passing through Jericho, a man named Zacchaeus, one of the most influential Jews in the Roman tax-collecting business (and, of course, a very rich man), tried to get a look at Jesus, but he was too short to see over the crowds. So he ran ahead and climbed into a sycamore tree beside the road, to watch from there.

When Jesus came by he looked up at Zacchaeus and called him by name! "Zacchaeus!" he said. "Quick! Come down! For I am going to be a guest in your home today!"

Zacchaeus hurriedly climbed down and took Jesus to his house in great excitement and joy.

But the crowds were displeased. "He has gone to be the guest of a notorious sinner," they grumbled.

Meanwhile, Zacchaeus stood before the Lord and said, "Sir, from now on I will give half my wealth to the poor, and if I find I have overcharged anyone on his taxes, I will penalize myself by giving him back four times as much!"

Jesus told him, "This shows that salvation has come to this home today. This man was one of the lost sons of Abraham, and I, the Messiah, have come to search for and to save such souls as his."

LUKE 19:1-10, TLB

~ 40 ~

"Three times a day he got down on his knees and prayed..."

The call of God led a young man, Daniel, away from his homeland and into the service of at least three pagan kings. We know only a few details about his life, but what we know leaves us breathless. For the details are not trivial. They speak to issues of character and integrity that we seek today—in ourselves and in those who are our leaders.

No one was better under fire than Daniel. His analytical, prophetic, and leadership capacities were peerless. But, as sometimes happens, his brilliance and purity of life gained him bitter enemies. And in the midst of such adversity we learn most about his spiritual disciplines: specifically praying to his Heavenly Father three times a day. His custom was not to be discouraged by anyone, not even those who threatened him with an "appointment" with the lions.

What does Daniel have to say to us across the centuries? Never let the tidal wave of demands for your time and loyalty become so great that you have lost your prime moments for communion with your God. It is in the less complicated moments that we prepare ourselves for action when the lions roar.

❧

Look well to the fire in your own souls, for the tendency of the fire is to go out.

WILLIAM BOOTH

Now when Daniel learned that the decree had been published, he went home to his upstairs room where the windows opened toward Jerusalem. Three times a day he got down on his knees and prayed, giving thanks to God, just as he had done before.

DANIEL 6:10

~ *41* ~

The Word of God is living and active...

There is a certain kind of temperament that exults in collecting and using vast amounts of information in order to impress and even intimidate others of lesser intellectual capacity. This temperament can be found at times even among followers of Christ.

Most of us know someone who memorizes Scripture, who pastes his doctrines together with care, who is quick to correct others when he or she perceives that details of Scripture have been overlooked or misinterpreted. However, this vast store of spiritual knowledge appears to make little difference in the formation of this person's inner devotion, public expression of character, or compassion toward those who are weak or struggling.

While the study of Scripture is useful in forming strong intellectual depth, this is not its sole purpose—or even its primary value. Scripture is meant to invade the deeper parts of the human soul, where life's greatest choices are made. And we must let this happen. We must invite its total invasion.

When Scripture has done its deepest work—correcting, assuring, redirecting, informing—we become aware that something has changed. There is a quiet humility, a repentant spirit, a reluctance to judge others, a sensitivity toward those who are weak. These are the signs that Scripture has indeed gone through us.

❧

There is a story of a learned man who came to visit a rebbe. The scholar was no longer a young man—he was close to thirty—but he had never before visited with the rebbe. "What have you done all your life?" the master asked him.

"I have gone through the whole Talmud three times," answered the learned man.

"Yes, but how much of the Talmud has gone through you?" the rebbe inquired.

HESCHEL

For the word of God is living and active. Sharper than any double-edged sword, it penetrates even to dividing soul and spirit, joints and marrow; it judges the thoughts and attitudes of the heart. Nothing in all creation is hidden from God's sight. Everything is uncovered and laid bare before the eyes of him to whom we must give account.

HEBREWS 4:12-13

~ 42 ~

But Jonah ran away from the Lord...

All in all Jonah was probably not a bad prophet. Not the best of the lot, but certainly not the worst. When we meet him in the Scriptures, we quickly learn that he was in need of a basic theology lesson. He lacked an understanding of the omnipresence of Israel's God.

The idea that God is equally and powerfully present everywhere presents us with a stunning thought. There is no place in all of Creation where God's Word is not both valid and compelling. Somehow Jonah chose to forget this. By heading away from God's call to Nineveh and toward a place he thought to be on the other end of the world, Jonah seemed to think that he could outrun his obligation to obey.

We have all experienced the fading of a radio signal as we drive further and further away from the station's transmitter site. Did Jonah think this would happen as he sailed away to Tarshish? That Heaven's signal would grow weaker and free him up from the call to preach repentance to a people he thought deserved only vengeance?

There are times when Jonah's insufficient theology can also be found in us. Do we not sometimes leave the sanctuary after a time of rousing worship, forgetting that God is as present to us in the larger world as he was in the holy place? His call to us to be a holy, witnessing people is as real on the streets and workplaces of our cities as it is when we sing his praises in church.

❧

The church has surrendered her once lofty concept of God and has substituted for it one so low, so ignoble, as to be utterly unworthy of thinking, worshipping (people). This she has not done deliberately, but little by little and without her knowledge; and her very unawareness only makes her situation all the more tragic.

A.W. TOZER

The word of the Lord came to Jonah son of Amittai: "Go to the great city of Nineveh and preach against it, because its wickedness has come up before me."

But Jonah ran away from the Lord and headed for Tarshish.

JONAH 1:1-3A

~ 43 ~

He (Jesus) entrusted himself to him who judges justly.

The attitudes and conduct of our Lord were not controlled by events or people around him. He lived by his own counsel, or, shall we say, by virtue of the connection he had with his Heavenly Father.

Jesus was not oblivious to circumstances, but nothing could provoke him to react in a manner inconsistent with his character or his mission. Enemies or critics could taunt him with questions designed to discredit him, and he would patiently answer and let the truth be the arbiter of the dispute.

His friends occasionally sank into doubt. Many of them ran from him when the air was full of danger. But Jesus never threatened or humiliated them in their lowest moments. It simply was not his way.

On the cross, Jesus chose to pray words of forgiveness rather than condemnation upon his executioners. This marvelous self-control was not mere stoicism. It reflected a heart fully surrendered to the purposes of his Father, a will fully submitted to the call to be the Redeemer of the world.

When you are safe in the Father's care, you need not flail away and defend yourself from the petty attempts of those in your world who seek to discredit you. A closed mouth, a purposeful mind, a heart attuned to his guidance is all one needs.

❧

When you are in the right, you can afford to keep your temper; when you are in the wrong, you cannot afford to lose it.

ON THE WALL OF GANDHI'S HOME IN SEVAGRAM

To this you were called, because Christ suffered for you, leaving you an example, that you should follow in his steps.

"He committed no sin,
and no deceit was found in his mouth."

1 PETER 2:21-22

~ 44 ~

He ... began to wash his disciples' feet...

One day Gandhi was approached by a proud young man who had recently earned a doctoral degree in economics. He loudly complained that he had been assigned a menial task in the life of the community. "Don't you realize that I am capable of big things?" he said to Gandhi, in the hope that he would be relieved of his chore and provided a task of greater dignity.

"I have no doubt that you are capable of big things," replied the great leader. "What I do not know is if you are capable of small things."

The Son of God was capable of great and small things. Whether it was washing feet (a menial job) or filling five thousand stomachs (perhaps a more significant one), everything our Lord did was done out of a heart of love.

Foot washing or similarly "small" tasks done merely to create an impression of humility are meaningless. But when the love of Christ fills our hearts and causes us to express that devotion to others, then we are on the path to true godliness.

❧

Towels and dishes and sandals, all the ordinary sordid things of our lives, reveal more quickly than anything what we are made of. It takes God Almighty Incarnate in us to do the meanest duty as it ought to be done.

OSWALD SANDERS

Jesus knew on the evening of Passover Day that it would be his last night on earth before returning to his Father. During supper the devil had already suggested to Judas Iscariot, Simon's son, that this was the night to carry out his plan to betray Jesus. Jesus knew that the Father had given him everything and that he had come from God and would return to God. And how he loved his disciples! So he got up from the supper table, took off his robe, wrapped a towel around his loins, poured water into a basin, and began to wash the disci-ples' feet and to wipe them with the towel he had around him.

When he came to Simon Peter, Peter said to him, "Master, you shouldn't be washing our feet like this!"

Jesus replied, "You don't understand now why I am doing it; some day you will."

JOHN 13:1-7, TLB

~ 45 ~

Abram built an altar to the Lord.

Abraham was called "the father of all who believe." This is a remarkable title and suggests, first of all, that Abraham's genuineness of faith was acceptable to God and would result in unusual blessing. Secondly, that Abraham's faith is a model to all of us: live in the pattern of Abraham life, and you move in the right direction.

We must never forget, however, that Abraham grew in his faith while living in Canaan, a part of the world known for its supreme cultural wickedness. Humanly speaking, Abraham was on his own. He had no one who could be for him a reliable source of spiritual strength and companionship.

It can be tempting to think that if we immerse ourselves in Christian culture—work and associate only with Christian organizations, actively participate in church programs, and listen incessantly to Christian media (sermons, books, Bible studies, etc.), we will automatically become more Christlike. The Scriptures do not back that up. Godly men and women, like Abraham, develop their spiritual muscle-power in the tough places.

When Abraham needed strength to enlarge the holy way, he simply built an altar. A holy place in a dark land. There in the midst of all the evil, he and God connected. And when the moment was finished, Abraham was a man enlarged in his faith, prepared to move forward.

એરુ

It is only by living completely in this world that one learns to live by faith.... By this worldliness I mean living unreservedly in life's duties, problems, successes and failures, experiences and perplexities.

DIETRICH BONHOEFFER

The Lord said to Abram after Lot had parted from him, "Lift up your eyes from where you are and look north and south, east and west.... Go, walk through the length and breadth of the land, for I am giving it to you."

So Abram moved his tents and went to live near the great trees of Mamre at Hebron, where he built an altar to the Lord.

GENESIS 13:14, 17-18

~ 46 ~

But even if I am poured out...
I am glad and rejoice with you all.

As we read in this passage, the Apostle Paul gave everything
he had in his quest to see men and woman brought under
the lordship of Jesus Christ and shepherded toward the
maturity of Christ-likeness. No sacrifice was too great—even
if it meant physical hardship or imprisonment. Though it
would ultimately mean his own martyrdom, Paul was ready
to go the distance.

What do we know of such urgency? What should we
know?

We speak of old-fashioned revival, and express our desire
that God would visit us with the refreshing power of his presence. But how could we expect that to happen until he finds
some of us ready to lay all at his feet—even our bodies?

❧

Let me say that if you are tired of demonstrations, I am tired of demonstrating. I am tired of the threat of death. I want to live. I don't want to be a martyr. And there are moments when I doubt if I am going to make it through. I am tired of getting hit, tired of being beaten, tired of going to jail. But the important thing is not how tired I am; the important thing is to get rid of the conditions that lead us to march.

Now gentlemen, you know we don't have much. We don't have much money. We don't really have much education, and we don't have political power. We have only our bodies, and you are asking us to give up the one thing that we have when you say, "Don't march."

MARTIN LUTHER KING
TO THE CHICAGO CITY COUNCIL

But even if I am being poured out like a drink offering on the sacrifice and service coming from your faith, I am glad and rejoice with all of you.

PHILIPPIANS 2:17

~ 47 ~

Lord, who may dwell in your sanctuary?

We have reached a new level of spiritual life when we hunger for holiness: being in the likeness of the one who saved us at the cross.

Holiness does not come through the drinking of a magic potion or seeking some religious experience. It is not normally learned at schools, from books, or in attendance at special conferences.

Rather, holiness is acquired, first, by seeking the Lord in the quiet hours. In those moments where distraction is lessened, we meditate on his character and personality. We brood on his words, his treatment of the weak, his rebukes to friends and critics. We see him suffer and ask ourselves, what qualities does he show in those painful moments.

We plan our day with the intent that all our choices, transactions, and behaviors (hidden or public) will carry his trademark of attitude and behavior. And then we ask the Spirit to empower our spirit—that these intentions might be fulfilled in the hours ahead.

At the end of the day we look backward acknowledging failure, giving thanks for success, joyfully remembering those moments when he was unusually present. As these things are done each day, holiness grows. Perhaps we are not aware of it, but others are, and they are drawn to Christ as a result.

❧

The best way to approach the study of holiness is not first to seek a definition (which is doomed from the start to be inadequate), but to gaze steadily and long at those in whom, by general consent, this quality appears....

Let him gaze most of all at Jesus Christ. Let him examine the lives of the saints. Let him think on those obscure disciples he has met on the road of life who seemed always to have the breath of God about them. Let him be unhurried and teachable.

And he will find that, far from holiness repelling him, it will fascinate and awe and subdue him. He will wonder at all God can do with human nature, and sink to his knees in marvel and surprise ... and he will catch himself shaping the question: "Even me?"

W.E. SANGSTER

Lord, who may go and find refuge and shelter in your tabernacle up on your holy hill?

Anyone who leads a blameless life and is truly sincere. Anyone who refuses to slander others, does not listen to gossip, never harms his neighbor, speaks out against sin, criticizes those committing it, commends the faithful followers of the Lord, keeps a promise even if it ruins him, does not crush his debtors with high interest rates, and refuses to testify against the innocent despite the bribes offered him— such a man shall stand firm forever.

PSALM 15, TLB

~ 48 ~

Let us keep in step with the Spirit...

The essential culture of the Christian community can be summed up with nine simple terms: love, joy, peace, patience, kindness, goodness, faithfulness, gentleness, and self-control.

For each of us, one or two of these qualities may be, more or less, natural, built in to our temperament. On the other hand, one or two of these qualities may be unnatural to us, even illusive. But each of these qualities is important. Together, they are the evidences that the Spirit of God lives within us. Living within, the Spirit desires to press these attributes into our character and personality.

We must assess ourselves regularly looking for signs that these qualities are present in us. "Last night I read through the fruits of the Spirit," a friend once said. "I discovered that I am not a very kind man." He models the effort and candor that each of us must undertake.

❧

This seems a cheerful world, Donatus, when I view it from this fair garden under the shadow of those vines. But if I climbed some great mountain and looked out over the wide lands, you know very well what I would see. Brigands on the high road, pirates on the seas, men murdered in the amphitheaters to please the applauding crowds, under all roofs misery and selfishness. It is really a bad world, Donatus, an incredibly bad world.

Yet in the midst of it I have found a quiet and holy people.

They have discovered a joy which is a thousand times better than any pleasures of this sinful life. They are despised and persecuted, but they care not. They have overcome the world. These people, Donatus, are the Christians ... and I am one of them.

ST. CYPRIAN TO DONATUS

I advise you to obey only the Holy Spirit's instructions. He will tell you where to go and what to do, and then you won't always be doing the wrong things your evil nature wants you to....

But when you follow your own wrong inclinations your lives will produce these evil results: impure thoughts, eagerness for lustful pleasure, idolatry, spiritism (that is, encouraging the activity of demons), hatred and fighting, jealousy and anger, constant effort to get the best for yourself, complaints and criticisms, the feeling that everyone else is wrong except those in your own little group—and there will be wrong doctrine, envy, murder, drunkenness, wild parties, and all that sort of thing. Let me tell you again as I have before, that anyone living that sort of life will not inherit the king-dom of God.

But when the Holy Spirit controls our lives he will produce this kind of fruit in us: love, joy, peace, patience, kindness, goodness, faithfulness, gentleness and self-control; and here there is no conflict with Jewish laws.

Those who belong to Christ have nailed their natural evil desires to his cross and crucified them there.

If we are living now by the Holy Spirit's power, let us follow the Holy Spirit's leading in every part of our lives.

GALATIANS 5:16, 19-25, TLB

~ 49 ~

And they were all filled with the Holy Spirit and spoke the word boldly.

The first generation of believers included no celebrities or superstars. No one stood out as having native brilliance or organizational ability. If there were people of exorbitant wealth, we know nothing about them. What we have in that first collection of Christ-followers, in actuality, is as common and as average a group of human beings as one could imagine.

But the power of their lives and their words shook a city, then a region, and finally a world. The secret: they were all filled with the Holy Spirit. Nothing else accounts for their awesome power. All the psychological, sociological, organizational, and economic explanations put together will not suffice to explain the dynamism of the first Christians.

Today it has been popular for some to say that if the Holy Spirit were to be lifted from the modern church, little if anything would change. If this is true, it is said to our shame. And it calls us to reevaluate our priorities as individuals and as a spiritual community. Have we given ourselves to elegant buildings and brilliantly constructed programs only to discover that our priorities were misplaced? For when the Holy Spirit fills a collection of Christ-followers, the result is vision, elevated character, intense and edifying fellowship, service to the larger world, growth in the number of believers.

What does it take to recover the power of those first believers? A prayer life like theirs, humility like theirs, love like theirs, and commitment to Jesus like theirs.

એરે

One of the commonest illusions of our day is that the individual is helpless, unable to do anything to alter events around him. Seeing the allegedly powerful so often at a loss, the ordinary man concludes that external forces are too strong for him and lapses into a "helplessness" syndrome.

This syndrome is particularly cruel because it drains the meaning out of life. Without a vision the people perish, sunk in a slough of comfort, frustration, or self-concern. Much of the mindless violence of our time stems from this sense that nothing constructive can be done.

GARTH LEAN

As soon as they were freed, Peter and John found the other disciples and told them what the Council had said.

Then all the believers united in this prayer:

"O Lord, Creator of heaven and earth and of the sea and everything in them—you spoke long ago by the Holy Spirit through our ancestor King David, your servant, saying, 'Why do the heathen rage against the Lord, and the foolish nations plan their little plots against Almighty God? The kings of the earth unite to fight against him, and against the anointed Son of God!'

"That is what is happening here in this city today! For Herod the king, and Pontius Pilate the governor, and all the Romans—as well as the people of Israel—are united against Jesus, your anointed Son, your holy servant. They won't stop at anything that you in your wise power will let them do. And now, O Lord, hear their threats, and grant to your servants great boldness in their preaching, and send your healing power, and may miracles and wonders be done by the name of your holy servant Jesus."

After this prayer, the building where they were meeting shook and they were all filled with the Holy Spirit and boldly preached God's message.

ACTS 4:23-31, TLB

~ *50* ~

Abram lived in the land of Canaan.

Anyone familiar with the primary stories of the Bible knows of Abraham and Lot. Though they were related, the two men reached a point where their business interests—sheep—conflicted with family unity. A separation became necessary. Decisions had to be made.

That Abraham was becoming an increasingly "converted" man to God's ways is evidenced in his method of solving the problem. The old Abraham, controlled by earlier cultural habits, would have insisted on pulling rank as the elder and picking the most promising territory (business-wise) for himself. But this was a new man, and he offered Lot the first choice. Result: Lot did the predictable, taking the lower, more promising plains, Abraham the hills of Canaan.

How difficult was this process for Abraham? The Scripture leaves us to our imaginations. But one has to believe that Abraham went through some anxious moments. Every bone in his businessman's body must have rebelled as he saw Lot head toward the verdant grasses of the valley. But Abraham also knew that Sodom lay just over the horizon.

We know that Abraham's way was vindicated. His family was established; Lot's family was virtually obliterated. His walk with God was enlarged; Lot's was diminished. His reputation and character were enhanced; Lot's was devastated. It all began with a decision to sacrifice his own best interests.

❧

The successful person has the habit of doing the things failures don't like to do. They don't like doing them either necessarily. But their disliking is subordinated to the strength of their purpose.

E.M. GRAY

And quarreling arose between Abram's herdsmen and the herdsmen of Lot. The Canaanites and Perizzites were also living in the land at that time.

So Abram said to Lot, "Let's not have any quarreling between you and me, or between your herdsmen and mine, for we are brothers. Is not the whole land before you? Let's part company. If you go to the left, I'll go to the right; if you go to the right, I'll go to the left."

GENESIS 13:7-9

~ *51* ~

Unless you forgive your brother from your heart...

Most of us have to engage in the action of forgiveness several times a day. Occasionally the forgiving takes enormous courage, for we have been greatly offended or betrayed. On most occasions, the forgiving is almost unconscious in execution. A driver cuts us off in traffic. How do we respond? Someone steps ahead of us in line. How do we handle the moment? An associate snaps at us in a tense conversation. What do we say in response?

The two most obvious reactions are exact opposites: forgiveness or retaliation.

How often must I forgive? Peter asks the Lord, offering his own answer. Seven times? It must have seemed at the time a very generous number. And it must have occurred to Peter that on the eighth occasion he would be free to take whatever action he deemed appropriate. Thus, he may not have been ready when the Savior told him that the number was seventy-seven times—a number that symbolized infinity.

The message could not be misunderstood. There is no room for retaliation in the Christian way. Grace is the way. Always grace.

❧

Clara Barton, the founder of the American Red Cross, had a well-known reputation as someone who never held a grudge. Once, when a friend reminded her of a wrong done to her some years earlier, she seemed not to know what her friend was talking about. "Surely you must remember!" said the friend.

"No," Clara replied without hesitation. "I distinctly remember forgetting that."

Then Peter came to Jesus and asked, "Lord, how many times shall I forgive my brother when he sins against me? Up to seven times?"

Jesus answered, "I tell you, not seven times, but seventy-seven times."

MATTHEW 18:21-22

~ 52 ~

Be transformed...

It is the mark of a saint not to permit the circumstances of the public world to dictate what will prevail in the privacy of the soul. There is always a choice to be made. Either the world will shape us, or we will shape it. What is it going to be?

When times are difficult, our natural instinct is to whine, or lapse into self-pity, or seek comfort in food, shopping, entertainment, and a thousand other options. Those who witness our journey (see Heb 12:1) would not stand for this. They have always chosen the higher way. Through the power of the Spirit they established a quality of calmness and courage in the heart. They identified with the sufferings of the Savior. And they reminded themselves that in such moments of harshness there is usually an opportunity to grow and to give witness to God's grace.

Seeking God's power, they endured and persevered. This too, on certain occasions, is our opportunity.

❧

About a night spent in a filthy jungle hut, Mary writes: "I am not very particular about my bed these days, but as I lay on ... dirty corn-shells, with plenty of rats and insects, three women and an infant three days old alongside, and over a dozen sheep and goats and cows outside, you don't wonder that I slept little. But I had such a comfortable quiet night in my own heart."

FROM THE JOURNAL OF
MARY SLESSOR

Do not conform any longer to the pattern of this world, but be transformed by the renewing of your mind. Then you will be able to test and approve what God's will is—his good, pleasing and perfect will.
ROMANS 12:2

~ 53 ~

Then I heard every creature in heaven and on earth ... singing.

Heard while leaving church: "Worship is such a drag ..." The response: "Yeah, it sure is, isn't it?"

How could this be? How could this hour (or more) that is supposed to be the most uplifting event of the week sink so low? How can it be that approaching the throne of heaven has become something so out of touch with our emotions, our minds, and our hearts that it has become irrelevant?

Worship should be *beautiful*, speaking to our love of beauty. But this does not mean it has to be a staged production worthy of Broadway. Worship should be *thoughtful*, feeding our intellectual hungers. But this does not mean that it should be turned into a lecture hall. Worship should be *life-renewing*, responding to our feelings of fatigue and failure. But this does not mean that it becomes a group therapy session. Worship should be *invigorating*, filling us with enthusiasm and vision. But this does not mean it has to be a pep rally. Worship should be *reverential*, reminding us that we are in the presence of the Everlasting God. But that does not mean it must be like a funeral.

When God's people (individually or as a congregation) genuinely worship, their actions should be a power, a magnificence, a depth, and a hopefulness that leaves spectators awestruck with the beauty of it all. One could not imagine life to be complete without it. Why should we be satisfied with anything less?

❧

(When Vladimir, Prince of Kiev, sent some of his people in search of true religion, some went to the Church of the Holy Wisdom in Constantinople. When they returned, they were reported to have said this to the prince about their experience.) "We knew not whether we were in heaven or on earth, for surely there is no such splendor or beauty anywhere upon earth. We cannot describe it to you: only this we know, that God dwells there among men, and that their service surpasses the worship of all other places. For we cannot forget that beauty."

ROBERT WEBBER

Then I looked and heard the voice of many angels, numbering thousands upon thousands, and ten thousand times ten thousand. They encircled the throne and the living creatures and the elders. In a loud voice they sang:

"Worthy is the Lamb, who was slain, to receive power and wealth and wisdom and strength and honor and glory and praise!"

Then I heard every creature in heaven and on earth and under the earth and on the sea, and all that is in them, singing:

"To him who sits on the throne and to the Lamb be praise and honor and glory and power, for ever and ever!"

The four living creatures said, "Amen," and the elders fell down and worshiped.

REVELATION 5:11-14

~ 54 ~

Feed my lambs.

After all his promises to be faithful to Jesus, the resolve of Simon Peter had collapsed at almost the first sign of a challenge. He had gone out into the night and wept bitter tears of personal defeat. Even after the resurrection, Simon had every reason to wonder how Jesus felt about his humiliating failure.

Question: Would there be a moment when Jesus would offer him a sharp rebuke and turn away from him?

We ask this because it is how we might expect to be treated in a similar circumstance. Perhaps more to the point, it is the way we would likely treat someone who has betrayed us.

But on this occasion it was not to be so. There on the beach at Galilee, Jesus put the humiliating moment behind them both. Just as Simon had betrayed the Lord three times, so now Jesus called him back to service three times: Feed my lambs; feed my sheep. Once again Jesus was entrusting his followers to Simon's future leadership.

Two simple messages here. The first: the love of Christ is restorative. It reaches toward those who are defeated and offers the second chance. Secondly, it calls us to do the same today toward those who have failed us. This is the hallmark of Christian love and grace.

❧

Aba Mios was asked by a soldier whether God would forgive a sinner. After instructing him at some length, the old man asked him: "Tell me, my son, if your cloak were torn, would you throw it away?"

"Oh, no!" the soldier replied. "I would mend it and wear it again."

The old man said to him, "Well, if you care for your cloak, will not God show mercy to his own creature?"

After breakfast Jesus said to Simon Peter, "Simon, son of John, do you love me more than these others?"

"Yes," Peter replied, "You know I am your friend."

"Then feed my lambs," Jesus told him.

Jesus repeated the question: "Simon, son of John, do you really love me?"

"Yes, Lord," Peter said, "you know I am your friend."

"Then take care of my sheep," Jesus said.

Once more he asked him, "Simon, son of John, are you even my friend?"

Peter was grieved at the way Jesus asked the question this third time. "Lord you know my heart; you know I am," he said.

Jesus said, "Then feed my little sheep."

JOHN 21:15-17, TLB

~ 55 ~

We have the mind of Christ.

The Christ-following life is not a call to mindlessness. It does not ask, for example, that we abandon rationality, neglect the arts, avoid the tough questions that, this side of heaven, seem to have no black-and-white answers.

The saints ought to sport the finest of minds. They should be disciplined to think, capable of engaging in respectful and thoughtful discourse, driven by a healthy curiosity to discover and enjoy everything that can be found and appreciated in creation.

The follower of Christ is a master of searching questions, reader of substantial books, seeker of friendship with those who are wiser and smarter. The follower of Christ is not afraid to acknowledge that he or she doesn't know certain things, is always humbled and capable of awe in the face of great mysteries.

"We have the mind of Christ," St. Paul wrote, and in so saying, he rejected the intellectually empty or lazy mind. His notion of the renewed mind included a life of intellectual discipline, submitted to the One who embodied the way of truth.

❧

The man of action has the present, but the thinker commands the future from his study ...

OLIVER W. HOLMES

The man without the Spirit does not accept the things that come from the Spirit of God, for they are foolishness to him, and he cannot understand them, because they are spiritually discerned. The spiritual man makes judgments about all things, but he himself is not subject to any man's judgment: "For who has known the mind of the Lord that he may instruct him?"

But we have the mind of Christ.

1 CORINTHIANS 2:14-16

~ 56 ~

I have fought the good fight...

It is exciting to see in a young person a fervent intention to be an obedient servant of the Lord. We are drawn to the enthusiasm and the energy of this zealous confession of faith.

Unfortunately, something sad happens in too many cases. Enthusiasm dissipates and energy is exhausted as declarations of youth are forgotten. The generation who demonstrated in American streets, declaring that it would give itself to the world's renewal, has become absorbed in the gathering of money and the building of mega-mansions in the suburbs.

Keep your eye on the one who perseveres, who speaks and lives with fervency about his or her life's calling forty years after the fact. These "marathoners" have kept the faith and stuck to the course. To be sure, there has been fatigue, occasional failure, and substandard choices. But these persevering ones always return to the first love and the core of the call.

While audiences may love the words of intention, God loves the faithfulness of the plodder—the one who determines to endure to the end. Every day begins with a reaffirmation of the call to a godly life, a renunciation of sin, a resurgence of hope that Jesus may come again at any moment. One simple saint like this attracts more attention in heaven than a dozen others whose performance is ... well, just a performance.

❦

I have dwelt forty years practically alone in Africa. I have been thirty-nine times stricken with the fever. Three times I have been attacked by lions, and several times attacked by rhinoceri. But let me say to you, I would gladly go through the whole thing again if I could have the joy of again bringing the word Savior and flashing it into the darkness that envelops another tribe in Central Africa.

WILLARD HOTCHKISS
NINETEENTH CENTURY ENGLISH MISSIONARY

I have fought the good fight, I have finished the race, I have kept the faith. Now there is in store for me the crown of righteousness, which the Lord, the righteous Judge, will award to me on that day—and not only to me, but also to all who have longed for his appearing.

2 TIMOTHY 4:7-8

~ 57 ~

Stand firm in one spirit...

Have you ever felt ambushed by sorrow? We should antici-pate such experiences in this life. This is not a statement prompted by gloom or pessimism. No one walks life's road without the inevitable disappointments and failures.

Then why are we surprised? Unprepared? Thrown off course? Why do we sometimes become angry and embit-tered?

When Paul wrote to the Philippians and called them to stand firm, he knew that many of the people he was address-ing had spent a large part of their lives in the Roman mili-tary. They were conversant with adversity, with the surprise moment in battle when the unexpected happened. They understood that these were the times when the best qualities were evidenced in the soul of the soldier. And they wel-comed the occasion to prove their allegiance.

Paul expected the same of them in their journey of faith. He did not wish hardship upon them, but he knew that these are the times that transform us into men and women of God. "Make every challenging hour serve you, not enslave you," was his call. Some heard him, and that was how saints were made.

❧

When the great oak is straining in the wind, the boughs drink in new beauty, and the trunk sends down a deeper root on the windward side.

Only the soul that knows the mighty grief can know the mighty rapture. Sorrows come to stretch out spaces in the heart for joy.

EDWIN MARKHAM

Whatever happens, conduct yourselves in a manner worthy of the gospel of Christ. Then, whether I come and see you or only hear about you in my absence, I will know that you stand firm in one spirit, contending as one man for the faith of the gospel without being frightened in any way by those who oppose you. This is a sign to them that they will be destroyed, but that you will be saved—and that by God. For it has been granted to you on behalf of Christ not only to believe on him, but also to suffer for him, since you are going through the same struggle you saw I had, and now hear that I still have.

PHILIPPIANS 1:27-30

~ 58 ~

Be silent before me...

The busier our lives become, the more influential our jobs, the greater the demands placed upon us, the more important it is that we stop habitually and become quiet before the Lord. It is too easy for us to become immersed in the noise and distraction of the age. It becomes a habit of the mind. We are uncomfortable, for example, if there is not some audio sensation beating upon our ears and thus into our hearts.

God will not out-shout the sounds of our age. He often whispers, and only those who are quiet will hear him. He does not need to compete with other voices; he will not take a place among the "auctioneers" bidding for our attention. If we will not still ourselves, enter the sanctuary, prostrate ourselves before this King of Kings, then we shall live a lifetime of frenzy, having never once heard the assurance that we are loved by the One who made us.

❧

We need to find God and he cannot be found in noise and restlessness. God is the friend of silence. See how nature—trees, flowers, grass—grow in silence; see the stars, the moon and the sun, how they move in silence ... the more we receive in silent prayer, the more we can give in active life. We need silence to touch souls.

MOTHER TERESA

Listen in silence before me, O lands beyond the sea. Bring your strongest arguments. Come now and speak. The court is ready for your case.

Who has stirred up this one from the east, whom victory meets at every step? Who, indeed, but the Lord? God has given him victory over many nations and permitted him to trample kings underfoot and to put entire armies to the sword. He chases them away and goes on safely, though the paths he treads are new. Who has done such mighty deeds, directing the affairs of generations of mankind as they march by? It is I, the Lord, the First and Last; I alone am he.

ISAIAH 41:1-4, TLB

~ 59 ~

He often refreshed me.

God gives each of us a remarkable ability to influence one another. We can encourage and we can discourage. We can bring out the best in a person, and we can bring out the worst. We can tempt and seduce, or inspire and coach. We have the power to *bless* and the power to *curse.*

We see the cursing all the time. In traffic one driver wishes another ill will with a gesture or an angry word. One person speaks harshly to another, wounding that person's spirit for days. We can curse one another through neglect, through ridicule, through unrelenting criticism. Many a son or daughter has lived an entire lifetime with the scars of things said or done in childhood by a mother or father.

But we also see the capacity to bless. The same mouth that curses, when reformed, is also capable of affirming, offering encouragement, giving guidance, expressing love. An athlete responds to the cheers of a crowd, a preacher gathers steam as his congregation responds with genuine conviction, a child becomes more confident through the praise of a loved one, and sinners come to Christ because of the tenderness of those who care for their souls.

Through Christ-centered friendship we obtain strength and vitality. In bearing one another's burdens, in rebuking and affirming, in loving and serving, we build one another up. Together we become an indomitable body of people. Onesiphorus, who "often refreshed" Paul, was a great example of this kind of friend.

I love to view all my Christian friends as fuel. Having gathered you all together on my hearth, I warm myself at your fire and find my Christian love burn and glow.

CHARLES SIMEON, NINETEENTH CENTURY PASTOR
TO STUDENT-GUESTS IN HIS CAMBRIDGE HOME

May the Lord show mercy to the household of Onesiphorus, because he often refreshed me and was not ashamed of my chains.

2 TIMOTHY 1:16

~ 60 ~

They gave as much as they were able.

At the center of all the ideals holding together a community of Christ-followers is that of generosity. Remove that belief, and all other things deteriorate rather quickly. What's left is just another generic organization. A nice group, perhaps, but one bereft of the power and uniqueness that the Christian connection was meant to have.

Christianity is synonymous with generosity. It reveals a God who loved the world by *giving* his Son, the supreme gift of heaven. Christianity brings doctrine to life by demonstrating to us *generosity in the flesh* through the life of Jesus. And then Christianity calls people to generosity through the transforming power of the Holy Spirit. Wherever people are filled with the spirit, generosity is not far behind.

"Greed is good," intones a fictional business leader in a famous Hollywood movie. We recoil at this brash assertion, but when we look about at the system a larger world has created for itself, we see that we are not far—if we haven't actually arrived—from a way of life that actually incarnates this perspective.

Among our most powerful messages to a dying culture is the way of generosity. When the ancient world once saw the way Christians gave to one another and to those who were in need, they were drawn to the power of their faith. It is time for a similar revival of generosity today.

❧

In O. Henry's famous short story "The Gift of the Magi," the young wife has only $1.87 to buy her husband a gift, and Christmas is the next day. Impulsively she decides to sell her long, thick hair to buy him a chain for his treasured gold watch. At the same moment he (the husband) is selling the watch to buy his present for her—special combs for her beautiful hair.

BRENNAN MANNING

And now, brothers, we want you to know about the grace that God has given the Macedonian churches. Out of the most severe trial, their overflowing joy and their extreme poverty welled up in rich generosity. For I testify that they gave as much as they were able, and even beyond their ability.

2 CORINTHIANS 8:1-3

~ *61* ~

It has always been my ambition...

Life means very little without a purpose that is bigger than we are. To rise each morning with no better intention than to feed our appetites, accumulate a bit more wealth, and to seek out some novel pleasure will never be good enough.

We have been wired to seek higher things. We are giving evidence of this when we speak of making a difference or leaving a legacy.

The Bible offers the stories of a fistful of people who heard the call of God and, in response, gave themselves to purposes much higher than themselves. In some cases, it actually cost them their lives if not their social acceptance among their peers. But as they gave themselves, nonetheless, they were transformed. They died with the satisfaction that they had pleased their God, that others were connected to heaven because of their efforts, that a new generation was better equipped to face life because of what they'd done.

Now here is this same Scripture saying that we, too, have a call to a higher purpose. A person listens every day for that call, hears it, and moves forward accordingly. And life takes on a joy, acquires a power, experiences a satisfaction that can be found nowhere else.

❧

Make no little plans. They have no magic to stir men's blood and probably themselves will not be realized. Make big plans ... remembering that a noble logical diagram, once recorded, will never die, but long after we are gone, will be a living thing, asserting itself with ever-growing insistency.

DANIEL BURNHAM, ARCHITECT AND PLANNER

It has always been my ambition to preach the gospel where Christ was not known, so that I would not be building on someone else's foundation. Rather, as it is written:

"Those who were not told about him will see, and those who have not heard will understand."

ROMANS 15:20-21

~ 62 ~

Open your eyes ... look at the fields...

The fourth chapter of John's gospel captures a particularly instructive moment in the public life of Jesus. It offers a record of one of our Lord's longer conversations. The significance of the occasion is compounded by the fact that the conversation occurs between Jesus and a woman with a highly questionable moral reputation.

The result of their discussion eventuated in a clear change of life and perspective for her. "Come, see a man who told me everything I ever did," she tells the people of her village when she returns home. "Could this be the Christ?"

Suddenly a whole raft of people made curious by her claim rush to find him. Which is not good news for the disciples who have gone to find food and would prefer to eat rather than handle another crowd of people. Jesus' comment? *"Open your eyes...,"* which is to say, look at the people and *what they might become.* His comment seems to be both a rebuke and an instruction. They are concerned about a literal meal; he is more concerned for a spiritual harvest.

In the early stages of their apprenticeship with Jesus, the disciples never seemed to understand that Jesus was in the "people-business." Food, power, things, organizational structure, and leadership, vital to the disciples, were relatively unimportant to him. Hence their irritation when he took precious time to bless children, converse with a woman (as in this case), heal lepers, and deal with tax collectors.

It is a helpful exercise for us when we ask if our "eyes" are open. Do we know a harvest (as defined by Christ) when we see it? Or are we passing by one opportunity after another— people in need of the love of Christ through us—because we have other seemingly more important things to do?

⁊⁊

Some people want to live within the sound
   of church or chapel bell;
I want to run a rescue shop
   within a yard of hell.

C.T. STUDD

*Then Jesus explained: "My nourishment comes from doing the will of
God who sent me, and from finishing his work. Do you think the
work of harvesting will not begin until the summer ends four months
from now? Look around you! Vast fields of human souls are ripening all around us, and are ready now for reaping. The reapers will
be paid good wages and will be gathering eternal souls into the gran-
aries of heaven! What joys await the sower and the reaper, both
together! For it is true that one sows and someone else reaps. I sent
you to reap where you didn't sow; others did the work, and you
received the harvest."*

JOHN 4:34-38, TLB

~ 63 ~

Who of you by worrying can add a single hour to his life?

When Jesus looked into the hearts of the crowds who followed after him it must have seemed as if everyone was enveloped in anxiety. Frightened, worried, often frantic people who lived in a world where it was easy to obsess with the problems of poverty, disease, famine, and exploitation from authorities and power moguls.

Not that these were insignificant matters, but our Lord began to direct the crowds toward higher thoughts—issues of spiritual reality, something with which most of them had lost touch. "Seek *first* his kingdom and his righteousness, and all these (other) things will be given to you as well." In other words, stop groveling your way through life. Look higher and deeper to the kingdom purposes of your God, and life will begin to change.

This was a call to faith, a rearrangement of priorities. His challenge was one that would require spiritual courage and trust in his word. Some accepted his challenge; most backed off.

The struggle to determine what is truly important revives every morning when we awaken. Each day we decide once again what our priorities will be: a preoccupation with winning, accumulating, the search for another ounce of fun *or* setting forth to be a servant of the kingdom—making our worlds welcoming to Christ.

❧

Let temporal things serve your use, but the eternal be the object of your desire.

THOMAS À KEMPIS

"And why do you worry about clothes? See how the lilies of the field grow. They do not labor or spin. Yet I tell you that not even Solomon in all his splendor was dressed like one of these.... Therefore do not worry about tomorrow, for tomorrow will worry about itself. Each day has enough trouble of its own. "

MATTHEW 6:28-29, 34

~ 64 ~

Let us not be like others who are asleep...

Sometimes we are tempted to think of the spiritual journey as one in which we are entitled to a pain-free, success-assured, fail-safe adventure. But in our more discerning moments, we know better. While we are acquainted with moments of unutterable joy when we abound in blessings that go far beyond what we deserve, we also are aware that there can be tough moments when everything about life seems at risk. Ask those who are part of the persecuted church around the world.

The Christ-follower cultivates what Mitchell calls the "discipline of uncertainty." Meaning that we submit *all events* into his hands. *All events!* The blessed ones *and* the tough ones.

In difficult times we ask how things can be redirected and caused to bring glory to the Savior and growth to the follower. And in the favorable times we ask what can be learned, perpetuated, used to advance the honor of God. And in all times, we learn to lead with a thankful heart. The bottom line: events do not control us; we control their outcomes through God's grace and power.

Only one who is (Paul's words) alert and self-controlled, who looks at people and events through eyes of faith and love and hope can ever hope to achieve this discipline.

❧

We live our lives under the discipline of uncertainty. We never know what emergencies may be approaching, what commissions may be ripening, what chances may be on the way, what temptations may lie in ambush, ready to spring unawares.

FRED MITCHELL

You are all sons of the light and sons of the day. We do not belong to the night or to the darkness. So then, let us not be like others, who are asleep, but let us be alert and self-controlled.

1 THESSALONIANS 5:5-6

~ 65 ~

I saw the Lord ... high and exalted...

We must be careful not to assume that praise and worship
are the same thing. While we will want to engage in both in
our private and public devotion, we must not confuse them.

Praise is that joyful expression of thanksgiving to God for
who he is and what he has done. It is to God that we lift
praise. He is the only receiver of our expression. If we use
the act of praise to make ourselves feel good, if praise
becomes an intoxicating experience meant primarily to lift
our spirits, we may want to evaluate its genuineness. A rock
concert, a comedian's routine, an exciting sports contest may
do the same.

Worship, which includes praise, goes further and deeper.
Through prayer, through the reading of God's Word,
through giving, through honest confession of sin, we enter
God's presence. We are appropriately overwhelmed by a
sense of his majesty, and we are also dismayed by our sinfulness ... perhaps to the point of strong emotion and the
desire through confession to be restored to alignment with
him. We will know that we have worshipped, as did Isaiah, if,
in the end, we have heard him speak in the form of calling,
reassurance of our place in God's family, and a renewed love
and openness to those in our community of faith.

❧

Worship is to feel in your heart and express in some appropriate manner a humbling but delightful sense of admiring awe and astonished wonder and overpowering love in the presence of that most ancient Mystery, that Majesty which philosophers call the First Cause but which we call Our Father Which Art in Heaven.

A.W. TOZER

The year King Uzziah died I saw the Lord! He was sitting on a lofty throne, and the Temple was filled with his glory. Hovering about him were mighty, six-winged seraphs. With two of their wings they covered their faces; with two others they covered their feet, and with two they flew. In a great antiphonal chorus they sang, "Holy, holy, holy is the Lord of Hosts; the whole earth is filled with his glory." Such singing it was! It shook the Temple to its foundations, and suddenly the entire sanctuary was filled with smoke.

Then I said "My doom is sealed, for I am a foul-mouthed sinner, a member of a sinful, foul-mouthed race; and I have looked upon the King, the Lord of heaven's armies."

Then one of the seraphs flew over to the altar and with a pair of tongs picked out a burning coal. He touched my lips with it and said, "Now you are pronounced 'Not guilty' because this coal has touched your lips. Your sins are all forgiven."

ISAIAH 6:1-7, TLB

~ 66 ~

The surpassing greatness of knowing Christ Jesus my Lord...

When the converting power of Jesus Christ comes upon a life, things change. One's perspective on the world, for example. Things are now seen in new and different ways that were, perhaps, not ever observed before. One's sense of value is altered. There is respect for things formerly despised; appreciation and admiration for things previously thought worthless.

Where once we were arrogant and self-seeking, we are more apt to acquire a quietness of spirit, a desire to serve others even at our own expense. While in the past we might have sought our satisfaction in accumulation of things or endless amusement, we are now more anxious to be in alignment with God and his kingdom and whatever it takes to enlarge it.

Things change when placed under his lordship. And inexpressible joy is the result.

❧

I walked over Boston Commons before breakfast weeping for joy and praising God. Oh, how I loved! In that hour I knew Jesus, and I loved Him till it seemed my heart would break with love. I was filled with love for all His creatures. I heard the little sparrows chattering; I loved them. I saw a little worm wiggling across my path; I stepped over it. I did not want to hurt any living thing. I loved the dogs, I loved the horses, I loved the little urchins on the street, I loved the strangers who hurried past me, I loved the heathen—I loved the world.

SALVATION ARMY OFFICER, SAMUEL LOGAN BRENGLE,
THE MORNING AFTER HE WAS CONVERTED TO CHRIST

But whatever was to my profit I now consider loss for the sake of Christ. What is more, I consider everything a loss compared to the surpassing greatness of knowing Christ Jesus my Lord, for whose sake I have lost all things.

PHILIPPIANS 3:7-8

~ 67 ~

The heart ... who can understand it?

The biblical writers take us deep into the interior of a person's life. In the earliest pages, we are taught that there is a solid-state beauty to the first persons God created and set in a garden. "The two were naked and unashamed," Genesis says. The comment refers not to physical nakedness as much as to the total transparency of hearts: the perfect communion of human beings.

But all of that was devastated when "the two" became rebellious. Their harmony of life was lost, their hearts darkened. Of this greatest of all human tragedies, Jeremiah is led to say, "the heart is deceitful above all things *and beyond cure ...*"

In humanity's spiritual history we have gone from extreme beauty to an extreme of spiritual pollution that leaves the heart so corrupted that one is helpless to know what it will produce next in the way of thought, motivation, attitude.

These two perspectives of the heart call us, first, to a hopeful optimism: that the way we were created—*naked and unashamed*—is the way we will become when Jesus returns and makes all things new. And, secondly, we are called to a realistic pessimism: that the way we are today—hearts corrupted beyond comprehensibility—will produce little that can ever be pure unless the saving work of Jesus is appropriated through faith.

 ❧

In a letter to Lady Huntingdon (an outstanding eighteenth-century Christian), the Duchess of Marlborough (an ancestor of Churchill) wrote, "When I am alone, my reflections and recollections almost kill me. Now there is Lady France Saunderson's great rout (party) tomorrow night—all the world will be there, and I must go. I do hate that woman as much as I do hate a physician, but I must go, if for no other purpose than to mortify and spite her. This is very wicked, I know, but I confess all my little peccadilloes to you....

DALLIMORE

The heart is deceitful above all things and beyond cure. Who can understand it?
"I the Lord search the heart and examine the mind, to reward a man according to his conduct, according to what his deeds deserve."

JEREMIAH 17:9-10

~ 68 ~

The Lord was with Joseph...

What caused Joseph to find favor in the eyes of the pagan leaders of Egypt was not words but quality of life and work. The man's work resumé certainly catches one's attention. He is first a slave, then a prisoner (arrested on trumped up charges) and then "number two" man in the nation. Who can you think of that matches this climb to success?

"He prospered ..." is the candid comment of the Biblical story teller. He prospered "because the Lord was with him." The writer seems content to leave it at that. Nothing else needs to be explained.

When the Lord is with some one, what are you most likely to see? In Joseph's case you are likely to see character of person first: loyalty, trustworthiness, excellence of work, a passionate concern for the interests of his employer.

Joseph would not have gone far if his faith had been expressed only in words. It was in his day-to-day habits of work and relationship that he demonstrated that the Lord was with him. Some, thankfully not all, modern Christians do not think enough about this. They are not people of their word; their work is of marginal quality, their relationships are substandard, and they are not always aligned with the best interests of the one who is their employer. They should not be surprised that their words about faith have no credibility.

Whether we sweep streets or lead great companies, the call to Christ-followers is the same: do it all to the glory of God. This was Joseph's secret.

෪෨

Some people have greatness thrust upon them. Very few have excellence thrust upon them. They achieve it. They do not achieve it unwittingly, by "doing what comes naturally," and they don't stumble into it in the course of amusing themselves. All excellence involves discipline and tenacity of purpose.

JOHN GARDNER

When Joseph arrived in Egypt as a captive of the Ishmaelite traders, he was purchased from them by Potiphar, a member of the personal staff of Pharaoh, the king of Egypt. Now this man Potiphar was the captain of the king's bodyguard and his chief executioner. The Lord greatly blessed Joseph there in the home of his master, so that everything he did succeeded. Potiphar noticed this and realized that the Lord was with Joseph in a very special way. So Joseph naturally became quite a favorite with him. Soon he was put in charge of the administration of Potiphar's household, and all of his business affairs. At once the Lord began blessing Potiphar for Joseph's sake. All his household affairs began to run smoothly, his crops flourished and his flocks multiplied. So Potiphar gave Joseph the complete administrative responsibility over everything he owned. He hadn't a worry in the world with Joseph there, except to decide what he wanted to eat! Joseph, by the way, was a very handsome young man.

GENESIS 39:1-6, TLB

~ 69 ~

I will go to the king...

She was just a young woman, and the circumstances which
brought her to "such a time as this" were strange to say the
least. From the protective environment of an extended family
where there were people who provided loving protection, she
had gone to a palace and life as a queen. One could easily
understand if she admitted to more than a few moments of
anxiety as to what this arrangement of events meant, why she
should find herself in such a place where no one knew or
cared about *her* God.

And then one day she awakened to a challenge where her
life (and the life of all of her people) was at stake. At first she
demurred. She was not up to the task, she said. The timing
was all wrong. No one would listen to her. She was not in a
position, she insisted, to help. The excuses piled up.

But the word came back from her life-long mentor, "don't
dare to ignore the strong possibility that this is *your* hour—the
moment of God's call." The words overcame her reluctance.
Once past the moment of choice, she acted with consummate
nobility, and an entire generation of God's chosen people
were saved.

Why is the story of Esther passed on to us? Perhaps it is
because we never know when a similar moment may arise for
us. Perhaps the scale of our moment may be smaller in terms
of the way the world measures things. But not so in terms of
heaven's judgment. Every time we are obedient to the nudge
of the Spirit, every time we choose the uniqueness of Christ's
way, every time we put God's way ahead of our own, we have
fallen into line with the great young woman who abandoned
her life to a great call and said, "If I perish, I perish."

৵

Daring to do what is right,
Not what fancy may tell you.
Valiantly grasping occasions,
Not cravenly doubting—
Freedom comes only through deed,
Not through thoughts taking wings.

Faint not nor fear,
But go out through the storm and the action,
Trusting in God whose commandment you
	faithfully follow.
Freedom exultant will welcome your spirit
	with joy.

DIETRICH BONHOEFFER

Esther told Hathach to go back and say to Mordecai,
	"All the world knows that anyone, whether man or woman, who goes into the king's inner court without his summons is doomed to die unless the king holds out his golden scepter; and the king has not called for me to come to him in more than a month."
	So Hathach gave Esther's message to Mordecai.
	This was Mordecai's reply to Esther: "Do you think you will escape there in the palace, when all other Jews are killed? If you keep quiet at a time like this, God will deliver the Jews from some other source, but you and your relatives will die; what's more, who can say but that God has brought you into the palace for just such a time as this?"

ESTHER 4:10-14, TLB

~ 70 ~

(Herod) had James...put to death with the sword.

We must not be surprised if there are times when we are tempted to think that other powers have a greater control over events than does heaven. We see that good people are slandered, persecuted, even killed, and there seems to be no justice. We find ourselves sinking into doubt. What we have prayed for seems unanswerable; what we perceive to be in the best interests of Christ does not happen. And we are left wondering, perhaps tempted toward disbelief. The Savior himself warns us of such moments.

"In the world you shall have tribulation," Jesus warned. "But I have overcome the world..." he reminded his listeners. Just beyond the darkness is a blaze of light.

We have never been promised that good people will not die for Christ. Nor have we been told that all things will turn out to *our* immediate advantage. What we have been assured is that nothing exceeds his eternal power and purpose. That all things—even the death of James and the imprisonment of Peter—will be woven together to create a tapestry of redemptive purpose. Today's sorrows will become tomorrow's joys.

❧

Men did not possess him. Even the fellow who shot him. Shooting is a confession—this man is too strong for me. John was too much for the gunman who shot him. The man made a mistake—he thought he was going to eliminate John.

William Nagenda, who is now in heaven, used to say, "When Satan gets angry with us, he knocks us and we bounce on the ground like a tennis ball, then he gets more angry and bounces us the last time but we bounce to heaven and he does not see us again." That is what the gunman did.

BISHOP FESTO KIVENGERE
PREACHING AT THE FUNERAL OF JOHN WILSON,
NOTED UGANDAN EVANGELIST
WHO WAS GUNNED DOWN AND DIED IN HIS WIFE'S ARMS

It was about this time that King Herod arrested some who belonged to the church, intending to persecute them. He had James, the brother of John, put to death with the sword. When he saw that this pleased the Jews, he proceeded to seize Peter also.

ACTS 12:1-3

~ 71 ~

They took note that these men had been with Jesus.

There are twin but opposing dangers in our perspective on Christian community. One is to think that the common, the uneducated person has nothing to say about life in God. The other is to think that our faith does not need the disciplines of the thoughtful, educated, learned scholar. There is a place of honor for both, and there is a need for both.

The fact is that the majority of the first men picked to be part of Jesus' company were simple people. If there was an outstanding scholar among them, we do not know who he was. But let it not be forgotten that Saul of Tarsus, sometimes called the thirteenth apostle, was among the most brilliant and best taught of his generation.

To whom, then, do we listen when there is need for instruction, for guidance? Who can we trust to help us understand the Word of God?

First and foremost, we look at character. Does a person show forth in his words, in his choices, in his treatment of people (especially the weaker person), in his generosity the likeness of Christ?

Then we look for wisdom. Are his insights and conclusions about life such that we cannot miss the depth of his Heavenly perspective?

Then we notice as this person worships. Does the entirety of his being swell up into praise and humility before God?

Finally, we study this person as he serves. Is anything too lowly, too humbling for him to do? In public life does he seek advantage, credit, applause, or does he point all actions to the Savior?

When you see someone like this, you know that you are with a person who has been with Jesus, and you become confident that this person is worthy of your listening.

&

Both in history and in life it is a phenomenon by no means rare to meet with comparatively unlettered people who seem to have struck profound spiritual depths ... while there are many highly educated people of whom one feels that they are performing clever antics with their minds to cover a gapping hollowness that lies within.

HERBERT BUTTERFIELD

When they saw the courage of Peter and John and realized that they were unschooled, ordinary men, they were astonished and they took note that these men had been with Jesus.

ACTS 4:13

~ 72 ~

This will mean fruitful labor for me...

The ultimate goal for the Christian—this side of heaven—is to reach a point of personal equilibrium in which living or dying are equal options.

For Paul, dying meant the opportunity to be in the presence of Jesus. Living meant the opportunity to serve Jesus. "What I shall choose, I don't know..." he wrote. What a wonderful ambivalence!

Paul would have been incredulous that anyone should contemplate retirement. He would have demanded a definition. And if we had told him that retirement meant disengaging from a world of work in order to play, he would have been shocked, repelled. He could never imagine that a Christian might be drawn to a play-based life. Some play, some rest, some amusement? Of course? But as a way of life? Never!

But if we told him that retirement meant withdrawing from the production of income in order to invest ourselves in the work of the Kingdom, he would have smiled and offered a suggestion or two of places to go, people to serve, things to do.

For this was his life: to die working for the One who had called him to service. If he was free to move about, he would go to lands where the name of Christ had not yet been spoken. If he was to remain in prison—as he was when he wrote these lines—then he would touch the lives of soldiers and guards who came into his circles of influence. Was there ever a moment when this man was not consumed with a purpose, committed to the work of Christ? Probably not.

❧

Let me die working,
Still tackling plans unfinished, tasks undone
Clean to its end, swift may my race be run.
No lagged steps, no faltering, no shirking;
  Let me die working.

CHARLES COWMAN

For to me, living means opportunities for Christ, and dying—well,
that's better yet! But if living will give me more opportunities to win
people to Christ, then I really don't know which is better, to live or die!
Sometimes I want to live and at other times I don't, for I long to go
and be with Christ. How much happier for me than being here! But
the fact is that I can be of more help to you by staying!
  Yes, I am still needed down here and so I feel certain I will be stay-
ing on earth a little longer, to help you grow and become happy in
your faith; my staying will make you glad and give you reason to glo-
rify Christ Jesus for keeping me safe, when I return to visit you again.

PHILIPPIANS 1:21-26, TLB

~ 73 ~

Don't be afraid; from now on you will catch men.

We can only guess at the priority qualities Jesus was looking for as he chose his disciples. Whatever they were, they seem to differ with what we might have required in a disciple. Could we be blamed if we sought the evidences of a sharp mind, polished social skills, an appropriate skill package, abundant past experience, and (as they say) walk-on-water references?

It is hard to take what we know about the disciples and see that any of them had what it takes if these are the most important traits. Who seems the most unqualified of them all? Hard to answer, but you would certainly want to keep a man like Simon Peter on a short leash.

What of his behavior on the day described in this reading when Jesus boarded his boat and asked to be rowed out a few yards into deeper water where he could speak to the pressing crowd. One is tempted to suggest that Peter's only interest in assisting the Lord had to do with good advertising. But who knows what the fisherman had been thinking for the days previous to this moment?

The sermon ended, a command comes to Simon: *put your nets over the side.* Which Peter does reluctantly. There is a miracle! Fish swarm the nets. And when the nets are filled, the Lord has Peter's attention. The fisherman intuits that the miracle is for him, a message that he is in the presence of extraordinary power. But can this power which commands even the fish into a net change the life of a young, apparently volatile man?

Peter's initial answer is no. But Jesus says yes. And so the call comes: *follow me.* And the formerly-resistant Simon Peter capitulates instantly. Apparently, he was ready. All Jesus had to do was nudge him in the right direction. So, would you have picked him?

❧

A traveler in the Appalachian Mountains stopped to watch a craftsman who was producing magnificent wood carvings of small dogs. "How do you do that?" the visitor asked, obviously impressed with the quality of the work.

"I just cut away all that isn't dog," came the answer.

One day as he was preaching on the shore of Lake Gennesaret, great crowds pressed in on him to listen to the Word of God. He noticed two empty boats standing at the water's edge while the fishermen washed their nets. Stepping into one of the boats, Jesus asked Simon, its owner, to push out a little into the water, so that he could sit in the boat and speak to the crowds from there.

When he had finished speaking, he said to Simon, "Now go out where it is deeper and let down your nets and you will catch a lot of fish!"

"Sir," Simon replied, "we worked hard all last night and didn't catch a thing. But if you say so, we'll try again."

And this time their nets were so full that they began to tear! A shout for help brought their partners in the other boat and soon both boats were filled with fish and on the verge of sinking.

When Simon Peter realized what had happened, he fell to his knees before Jesus and said, "Oh, sir, please leave us—I'm too much of a sinner for you to have around." For he was awestruck by the size of their catch, as were the others with him, and his partners too—James and John, the sons of Zebedee. Jesus replied, "Don't be afraid! From now on you'll be fishing for the souls of men!"

And as soon as they landed, they left everything and went with him.

LUKE 5:1-11, TLB

~ 74 ~

Watch your life and doctrine closely.

The coach says to the athlete, "I intend to make your practices and your conditioning exercises so difficult that, by contrast, you will find the race a pleasure." The message is simple: practice the basics over and over, and, when the crisis comes, you will be prepared.

By nature most of us tend to reject this notion. We think of days in which nothing out of the ordinary happens as boring, non-contributive to our overall spiritual welfare. But it is in the quiet days that our souls are molded for the extraordinary moments of service.

In almost every one of the biblical biographies, we hear of only a handful of incidents which make those men and women great in our eyes. Rarely do we stop to think that in the intervening years when they shepherded sheep, raised families, engaged others in the life of the community that they were building the appropriate stamina for the sudden breakthroughs when they were called to do the noteworthy thing.

It is in the closet of prayer when the pressure is off, in the Holy Scriptures when all is quiet, in the little, unnoticed activities where we are routinely faithful that we build the spiritual muscle that makes us capable when the big battles break out.

❧

Someday, in years to come, you'll be wrestling with the great temptation, or trembling under the great sorrow, of your life. But the real struggle is here, now, in these quiet weeks. Now it is being decided whether, in the day of your supreme sorrow or temptation, you shall miserably fail or gloriously conquer. Character cannot be made except by a steady, long-continued process.

PHILLIPS BROOKS

At my first defense, no one came to my support, but everyone deserted me. May it not be held against them.

2 TIMOTHY 4:16

~ 75 ~

Oh, the depth of the riches of the wisdom and knowledge of God!

It is a frightful thought that our view of the majesty and power of God might not have developed since the day of simple childhood thoughts. We may not have been adequately encouraged to invite his presence and purpose in all our adult affairs: our work, our intellectual development, our primary relationships, the larger world of issues and opportunities.

This One who is our God and who is so expansive in wisdom and knowledge seeks access to every sector of our lives. He seeks to mold our thoughts and convictions, to press his presence into our actions (both simple and complex) so that we walk as if his sons and daughters. He calls us to deep and penetrating thinking (not simplistic or easy answers). He yearns that we might seek his glory in the creation, in the arts, in the world of the weak and the poor. He is prepared to reveal himself in the tiniest sub-atomic particle and the greatest galaxy millions of light years away ... and in everything else between.

৯৩

The trouble with many people today is that they have not found a God big enough for modern needs. While their experience of life has grown in a score of directions, and their mental horizons have been expanded to the point of bewilderment by world events and by scientific discoveries, their ideas of God have remained largely static.

J.B. PHILLIPS

Oh, the depth of the riches of the wisdom and knowledge of God!
  How unsearchable his judgments,
  and his paths beyond tracing out!
  "Who has known the mind of the Lord?
  Or who has been his counselor?"
  "Who has ever given to God,
  that God should repay him?"
  For from him and through him
  and to him are all things.
  To him be the glory forever!
  Amen.

ROMANS 11:33-36

~ 76 ~

Examine yourselves ... test yourselves.

The way to a mature knowledge of God and the way to an authentic, Christlike life begins with the humility of the repentant heart. Repentance is that sorrowful acknowledgement that a sinful and rebellious condition dwells within my innermost being. The repentant person is quite aware that, left to him or herself, any form of evil is possible.

Most of us would like to avoid this repentant perspective. We would much prefer to present ourselves to Christ under the assumption that he is fortunate to have us on his side. We would like to emphasize our progress in the faith, our spreading knowledge of his revelation. We would like to present a resumé of things accomplished for which others have given us applause and recognition.

One wonders if God does not sadly shake his head when we come toward him with such offerings. A galaxy-sized basket of such achievements would not begin to impress this One who welcomes sinners. For his hand is open not to the achiever but to the "repenter", the one who says, "Nothing in my hand I bring; simply to the cross I cling."

❧

To know myself, and especially as the wise man says, to know the plague of my own heart, is the true and the only key to all other true knowledge: God and man; the Redeemer and the devil; heaven and hell; faith, hope, and charity; unbelief, despair, and malignity, and all things of that kind;... all knowledge will come to the man who knows himself, and to that man alone.

ALEXANDER WHYTE

Examine yourselves to see whether you are in the faith; test yourselves. Do you not realize that Christ Jesus is in you—unless, of course, you fail the test?... For we cannot do anything against the truth, but only for the truth. We are glad whenever we are weak but you are strong; and our prayer is for your perfection.

2 CORINTHIANS 13:5, 8-9

~ 77 ~

Why are you sleeping?

We sometimes have moments of profound regret when we look back at certain events in our lives and realize that we completely misunderstood the significance of the hour. We spoke a word, made a choice, initiated an action, and all of life has changed as a result. And later we reflect: if I had only understood the implications of that moment.

It would be convenient if there was a little voice within that might say on occasion: *be careful what you do or say next. Your life (or someone else's life) will inexorably change as a result.* Unfortunately the voice, at least in that form, does not exist.

When the disciples chose to sleep in the Garden of Gethsemane rather than pray as Jesus challenged them, they did not know that, within an hour or two, they would face one of the greatest tests of their lives. Their choice to doze for a moment certainly caught them up on lost sleep. But the lack of prayer probably cost them courage and discernment, something much more needed when the persecutors came.

This is a dangerous day in which we live. Most dangerous, perhaps, because we tend to be insensitive to the accumulating spiritual implications of our choices. "Affairs are (indeed) now soul-sized." Meaning that many of the issues we face will either corrupt the soul or make it a dwelling place of God. We cannot afford to begin even one day without obeying Jesus' charge to the disciples who, to their peril, chose to ignore it: *Pray that you will not enter into temptation.* They slept and failed; he prayed and fulfilled his mission.

❧

Dead and cold we may be, but this
Is not winter now. The frozen miseries of centuries
Cracks, breaks, begins to move.
The thunder is the thunder of floes,
The thaw, the flood, the upstart spring.
Thank God, our time is now when wrong
Comes out to face us everywhere
Never to leave us till we take
The longest stride of soul men ever took,
Affairs are now soul size.

CHRISTOPHER FRY

Then, accompanied by the disciples, he left the upstairs room and went as usual to the Mount of Olives. There he told them, "Pray God that you will not be overcome by temptation."

He walked away, perhaps a stone's throw, and knelt down and prayed this prayer: "Father, if you are willing, please take away this cup of horror from me. But I want your will, not mine." Then an angel from heaven appeared and strengthened him, for he was in such agony of spirit that he broke into a sweat of blood, with great drops falling to the ground as he prayed more and more earnestly. At last he stood up again and returned to the disciples—only to find them asleep, exhausted from grief.

"Asleep!" he said. "Get up! Pray God that you will not fall when you are tempted."

LUKE 22:39-46, TLB

~ 78 ~

But even if you should suffer...

Not for a moment would any of us ask to suffer. But sooner or later we do. The godly person anticipates the best of all things and prepares for the worst.

And if the suffering hour should come, the follower of Christ immediately asks these questions:

1. Which of the Christian graces is needed for this hour?
2. How shall I hear God speak in this stressful time?
3. What can be learned that will be of value to others when the light comes?
4. How can the Spirit of Jesus be seen in me?

We are tempted to reserve the word *suffer* for moments of great magnitude: the debilitating illness, the loss of someone we love, the destruction of our possessions, a massive disappointment. But there are many sufferings, small adverse moments which come every day. Perhaps we overstate them by speaking of them as suffering. But call them what you will, they challenge us in the same way. And if we waste those moments, we lose out on the deepenings which are possible every time life turns tough.

❧

In the truest sense ... God is always leading us up and out of our darkest days into the larger service made possible by such a training time. Have we at the close of such periods quietly asked him what our next step should be, or have we tarried for a while to pity ourselves for the hard time we have had.

PHILIP HOWARD

Who is going to harm you if you are eager to do good? But even if you should suffer for what is right, you are blessed. "Do not fear what they fear; do not be frightened." But in your hearts set apart Christ as Lord. Always be prepared to give an answer to everyone who asks you to give the reason for the hope that you have. But do this with gentleness and respect.

1 PETER 3:13-15

~ 79 ~

Be very careful, then, how you live.

When the Christian message burst upon the world through the witness of the Apostles, it came in to a time where most people thought of their lives as insignificant and inconsequential. They assumed that, as individuals, they simply did not count.

Jesus Christ changed all such perceptions. By blessing children, calling common men to follow him, healing the outcasts, and restoring to fellowship those who had failed, he made it clear: *we belong to God*, we are given a special calling to participate in the building of his kingdom, and *we are valuable* (each equally with the other) in his sight.

This is both a liberating and a challenging Gospel. *Liberating* because it relieves us of the pressure to be a copy of someone else.

And *challenging* because I must resolve everyday to become more and more the person *God made me to be*. And this means *fighting* the spiritual "cancers" which would deny me the gift of abundant life. It means *yielding* to his Spirit in order that Christ's character might be built up in my life. And it means *obedience* whenever his call to Kingdom service is heard.

⁊⁊

There is a (story) told of a rabbi—Rabbi Zuscha. On his deathbed he was asked what he thought the kingdom of God would be like. The old rabbi thought for a long time; then he replied: "I don't really know. But one thing I do know: when I get there, I am not going to be asked, 'why weren't you Moses?' or 'why weren't you David?' I am going to be asked, 'why weren't you Zuscha?'"

BASIL PENNINGTON

Therefore, as God's chosen people, holy and dearly loved, clothe yourselves with compassion, kindness, humility, gentleness and patience. Bear with each other and forgive whatever grievances you may have against one another. Forgive as the Lord forgave you. And over all these virtues put on love, which binds them all together in perfect unity.

Let the peace of Christ rule in your hearts, since as members of one body you were called to peace. And be thankful. Let the word of Christ dwell in you richly as you teach and admonish one another with all wisdom, and as you sing psalms, hymns and spiritual songs with gratitude in your hearts to God. And whatever you do, whether in word or deed, do it all in the name of the Lord Jesus, giving thanks to God the Father through him.

COLOSSIANS 3:12-17

~ 80 ~

Let us run the race

We admire the winning athlete and, perhaps, fantasize for a moment that we are in their shoes. Truth be told, we sometimes envy the acclaimed scholar, the successful business person, the wise person who is consulted by many. And we wonder what it would take to become like them, to share in the fruits of their achievements.

If, in our curiosity, we study the lives of honorable and exceptional people, we will discover that there is a common truth at the root of all noble achievements. *Self-denial.* Outstanding people have learned to say "no" to the easy things of life and "yes" to the more substantial things. The athlete has trained while others have lazed away the day. The scholar has studied while others have sought amusement. The business person has worked the extra hours. And the wise person has deepened in insight through suffering and listening and thinking.

In similar ways we gaze upon that man or woman who walks with God. We love to be in their presence because they exhibit an extraordinary spiritual connection. When they pray, we know heaven has heard. When they touch lives, we know that people have felt genuinely loved. When there is a moment of chaos or confusion and they speak meaning into it, we know that they have offered a heavenly perspective.

There is no pill, no book with simple steps, no five-week course which paves the way to genuine Christian maturity. It is a pathway strewn with challenging choices, embraced suffering, difficult sacrifices, and the willingness to be humbled. Let's be candid: Many people would avoid this pathway. But for those who follow it, the results are magnificent. *Christlikeness!*

❧

Men are captivated with the idea of self-denial, and then they invent ingenious ways to make self-denial comfortable and easy.

PHILLIP BROOKS

Therefore, since we are surrounded by such a great cloud of witnesses, let us throw off everything that hinders and the sin that so easily entangles, and let us run with perseverance the race marked out for us. Let us fix our eyes on Jesus, the author and perfecter of our faith, who for the joy set before him endured the cross, scorning its shame, and sat down at the right hand of the throne of God. Consider him who endured such opposition from sinful men, so that you will not grow weary and lose heart.

HEBREWS 12:1-3

~ 81~

"My power is made perfect in weakness..."

The athlete speaks of being in the zone: that rare moment when nothing can go wrong. When all parts of the mind and body work together in perfect synchrony and the game of a lifetime is played.

Sooner or later the follower of the Lord experiences such a moment: when God seems so near, when all the thoughts of the mind are trained upon him, when we are in a frame of heart where we are willing to go anywhere, do anything, become whatever the Lord asks of us. And the sweetness of the moment is beyond description. We wish that we could preserve it, that it would never leave.

Usually we find that these are moments when our backs have been pinned against the wall, when we are weak in our own strength, strong in his. We would not have invited the weakness for anything. But it is here and God has offered us his presence.

❧

C.S. Lewis writes of a moment when all daily routines are suddenly interrupted by a stab of pain and the necessity of emergency medical treatment.

"At first I am overwhelmed and all my little happinesses look like broken toys. Then, slowly and reluctantly ... I remind myself that all these toys were never intended to possess my heart, that my true good is in another world and my only real treasure is Christ.... But the moment the threat is withdrawn, my whole nature leaps back to the toys: I am even anxious, God forgive me, to banish from my mind the only thing that supported me under the threat because it is now associated with the misery of those few days.... Let Him but sheathe that sword for a moment and I behave like a puppy when the hated bath is over—I shake myself as dry as I can and race off to reacquire my comfortable dirtiness, if not in the nearest manure heap, at least in the nearest flower bed. And that is why tribulations cannot cease until God either sees us remade or sees that our remaking is now hopeless.

C.S. LEWIS

To keep me from becoming conceited because of these surpassingly great revelations, there was given me a thorn in my flesh, a messenger of Satan, to torment me. Three times I pleaded with the Lord to take it away from me. But he said to me, "My grace is sufficient for you, for my power is made perfect in weakness." Therefore I will boast all the more gladly about my weaknesses, so that Christ's power may rest on me. That is why, for Christ's sake, I delight in weaknesses, in insults, in hardships, in persecutions, in difficulties. For when I am weak, then I am strong.

2 CORINTHIANS 12:7-10

~ 82 ~

Be still and know that I am God...

This oft-quoted phrase—be still and know that I am God—
may sometimes be misinterpreted. Perhaps it is not as much
a quiet invitation to stillness as it is a demand for silence
shouted by the conqueror to the conquered.

The words "be still" may actually be a reprimand such as a
parent might speak sharply to a child who is out of control
or a crowd that has become unruly. "Know that I am God"
may actually be directed toward the one who has no idea
who God is at all. *Be still and know that I am God* may be a
challenge to one who thought he or she knew just about
everything and had become accustomed to boasting about it.

But now God speaks, and it is time for all other mouths to
close. To be silent and face the fact that God is on the
throne of the universe. He has something to say, and we
must be still—out of obedience, out of reverence and
respect, out of personal need.

Silence is not native to my world. Silence, more than likely, is a stranger to your world too. If you and I ever have silence in our noisy hearts, we are going to have to grow it.... You can nurture silence in your noisy heart if you value it, cherish it, and are eager to nourish it.

WAYNE OATES

God is our refuge and strength, a tested help in times of trouble. And so we need not fear even if the world blows up, and the mountains crumble into the sea. Let the oceans roar and foam; let the mountains tremble!...

"Stand silent! Know that I am God! I will be honored by every nation in the world!"

The Commander of the heavenly armies is here among us! He, the God of Jacob, has come to rescue us!

PSALM 46:1-3, 10-11, TLB

~ 83 ~

"And do not grieve the Holy Spirit of God..."

We are called to a higher way of living. Our personal conduct is to resemble the pattern that Christ set for his disciples. More challenging still, perhaps, we are called to create a community with fellow-believers that emulates the love of Christ. The Christian "politic" is a rejection of the old vengeance-based politic of former cultures where one never forgot an offense and did what he could to extract retribution of a greater magnitude than that of the original deed.

Paul writes to Ephesian men and women, newly believing Greeks and Jews whose lives were in the process of dramatic transformation. Watch your talk, he writes. All conversation ought to be based upon causing others to grow. Rid your hearts of bitterness, rage, and anger. Forswear the right to get even either with words or physical force. Treat each other with kindness and compassion—uncommon behaviors in a Greek world, *actually considered to be on the weak side of human transactions.*

And then the most challenging of all: forgive one another (when offended) just as you have been forgiven. In other words renounce the right to get even, to punish, to extract a piece of pain equal to or greater than what was given to you. In the final analysis: choose to forget what has happened and keep forgetting every day.

Only when the Holy Spirit of God empowers a person can this be done. This is why we must ask to be filled with that Spirit every day.

❧

There is one sister in the community who has the knack of rubbing me up the wrong way at every turn; her tricks of manner, her tricks of speech, her character, strike me as unlovable. But then, she's a holy religious; God must love her dearly, so I wasn't going to let this natural antipathy get the best of me. I reminded myself that charity isn't a matter of fine sentiments; it means doing things. So I determined to treat this sister as if she were the person I loved best in the world. Every time I met her, I used to pray for her, offering to God all her virtues and her merits. I felt certain that Jesus would like me to do that.

THÉRÈSE OF LISIEUX

Get rid of all bitterness, rage and anger, brawling and slander, along with every form of malice. Be kind and compassionate to one another, forgiving each other, just as in Christ God forgave you.

EPHESIANS 4:31-32

~ 84 ~

"I knew you ... I set you apart ... I appointed you."

With these words, God called Jeremiah who became known as *the weeping prophet.* His was an unenviable task: to declare to the people of Jerusalem that God's patience had run out, that the consequences of generations of defiance were about to come clear. In responding to the call, Jeremiah would become enmeshed in the sufferings of the people: a good man sharing in the tragedies incurred by disobedient people.

Biblical people believe that the God of heaven calls men and women to kingdom service. For most of us, the call comes to accomplish things that will never be praised by others. Often we will be asked to be faithful to seeming "little things," the nuts and bolts of the kingdom of God.

Occasionally, however, a person is called from heaven to "stand in the gap," as Ezekiel once put it. The assignment is to confront kings or presidents or entire cities with a difficult word.

Some might envy the notoriety of a prophet. Don't! Prophets usually suffer. Prophets can often lose friends, careers, even (as in the experience of Jeremiah) their own lives.

Still others criticize prophets, thinking they know best what he (or she) should or shouldn't do or say. Again, don't! Until we have come under the discipline of their call, we had best pray for them.

We must begin each day with a heart to obey the calls to the little things. And we must begin each day ready, should God choose, to obey the call to stand in the gap, to be the prophet.

❧

So always do men speak who would make God a servant of their small concerns, an instrument at their disposal, a sort of divine insurance against loss or damage. Such men will always be disappointed in God. For they do not know that God is not at all at their service, but, quite the other way around, is summoning them to the service of his kingdom.

JOHN BRIGHT

The word of the Lord came to me, saying,
   "Before I formed you in the womb I knew you,
   before you were born I set you apart;
   I appointed you as a prophet to the nations."
   "Ah, Sovereign Lord," I said, "I do not know how to speak; I am only a child."
   But the Lord said to me, "Do not say, 'I am only a child.' You must go to everyone I send you to and say whatever I command you. Do not be afraid of them, for I am with you and will rescue you," declares the Lord.
   Then the Lord reached out his hand and touched my mouth and said to me, "Now, I have put my words in your mouth. See, today I appoint you over nations and kingdoms to uproot and tear down, to destroy and overthrow, to build and to plant."

JEREMIAH 1:4-10

~ 85 ~

When I want to do good...

A larger world likes to win our attention to the *outer things*. Our appearance, our wealth, our achievements, our charm. But this is not who we are. The person we are in actuality is first found deep within. Few, if any, will know this person deep within us; perhaps we ourselves are even confused at times about the person within.

What of those times when thoughts and intentions reach the surface of our lives and surprise us as much as they do others. We hear ourselves say, "I'm not sure I even know the one inside of me who came up with that."

The man or woman who would be faithful to God is careful to take the necessary time to monitor the "central stream of what we are indeed." From that interior part will come the issues most likely to betray us and grieve the Savior. But from that interior part, also, is likely to come the quiet voice of the indwelling Lord who reassures, who rebukes and affirms, who pokes and prods us on to better things.

In Paul's case a look within brought initial frustration but was followed by certain assurance: *Who will rescue me from this body of death? (This stranger within?) Thanks be to God—through Jesus Christ our Lord.*

❧

Below the surface-stream, shallow and light
  Of what we *say* we feel—below the stream
As light of what we *think* we feel—there flows
  With noiseless current strong, obscure and deep
The central stream of what we are indeed.

MATTHEW ARNOLD

*I know that nothing good lives in me, that is, in my sinful nature.
For I have the desire to do what is good, but I cannot carry it out.
For what I do is not the good I want to do; no, the evil I do not want
to do—this I keep on doing.*

*What a wretched man I am! Who will rescue me from this body of
death? Thanks be to God—through Jesus Christ our Lord!*

*So then, I myself in my mind am a slave to God's law, but in the
sinful nature a slave to the law of sin.*

ROMANS 7:18-19, 24-25

~ 86 ~

So (Elijah) got up and ate and drank.

Ours is not an impractical God. Nor is God one who is harsh or stingy. And, furthermore, he does not limit himself to mere religious expressions of grace and kindness.

When Elijah was engulfed in mental and spiritual exhaustion—we might even call it depression—the last thing the man needed was a sermon or a theology course. He needed no church service, no books on spiritual self-help.

What he needed was rest, food, and a refreshing drink. And God saw to it that he got all three. A God who cares like this might also know when we need a good laugh, a day in the countryside, a stimulating book, an embrace and a kiss. Perhaps this God of ours sometimes even whispers to us in words a modern person understands, "lighten up!"

If only we could appreciate this dimension of Elijah's God. Then we might become more aware that he is Lord of the whole person, the One who delights when his people discover that life is meant to be marked with joy and renewal ... even fun.

❧

Cardinal Basil Hume once spoke of a boyhood moment when his mother found him with a hand in the cookie jar. She suggested that God might see him and be angry with him. But now the Cardinal looks back on the moment and says that he expects that when he meets God on that coming day, he will hear the heavenly Father say, "Basil, why didn't you take two?"

So Elijah fled for his life; he went to Beer-sheba, a city of Judah, and left his servant there. Then he went on alone into the wilderness, traveling all day, and sat down under a broom bush and prayed that he might die.

"I've had enough," he told the Lord. "Take away my life. I've got to die sometime, and it might as well be now."

Then he lay down and slept beneath the broom bush. But as he was sleeping, an angel touched him and told him to get up and eat! He looked around and saw some bread baking on hot stones, and a jar of water! So he ate and drank and lay down again.

Then the angel of the Lord came again and touched him and said, "Get up and eat some more, for there is a long journey ahead of you."

So he got up and ate and drank, and the food gave him enough strength to travel forty days and forty nights to Mount Horeb, the mountain of God, where he lived in a cave.

But the Lord said to him, "What are you doing here, Elijah?"

1 KINGS 19:3-9, TLB

~ 87 ~

Return to me with all your heart.

We must never engage in the act of repentance in a cavalier fashion. One might do well to become spiritually cautious if one finds that too many prayers contain the overused words, *forgive me for my sins,* and nothing more.

Genuine repentance is the central and most significant act in restoring us to God and initiating deep change in life. When heaven hears the cry of the repentant person, it springs into action and unleashes the forgiving power of the atonement upon the one who has acknowledged sin and sinfulness.

Heaven does not ask for a specific set of words, nor a ceremony attended by robed clergy. Neither does heaven quibble about one's ideology or past. Heaven knows only one thing: the authentic sorrow of the heart expressed in concrete words. "For I am a man of unclean lips, and I live among a people of unclean lips," Isaiah said in repentance. So saying, Isaiah owned up to a life where he had taken God's laws lightly and had worried little about offending him. It was this transparency which endeared him to the Father and eventuated in his call to become one of the greatest of all the prophets.

When we return in repentance to God, he is quick to forgive, to restore, to bring a new thing into motion.

❧

We do not confess our faults in order that God may be better acquainted with them, but in order that the concreteness of words will increase our own understanding. The psalmist said, "Even before a word is on my tongue, lo, O Lord, thou knowest it all together."

ELIZABETH O'CONNOR

> *"Even now," declares the Lord,*
>> *"return to me with all your heart,*
>> *with fasting and weeping and mourning."*
> *Rend your heart*
>> *and not your garments.*
> *Return to the Lord your God,*
>> *for he is gracious and compassionate,*
> *slow to anger and abounding in love,*
>> *and he relents from sending calamity.*
> *Who knows? He may turn and have pity*
>> *and leave behind a blessing—*
> *grain offerings and drink offerings*
>> *for the Lord your God.*

JOEL 2:12-14

~ 88 ~

Anyone who does not take his cross and follow me is not worthy of me.

For all the talk we hear about how comforted one might be in relationship to Jesus, there is another sense in which we are seriously discomforted ... or should be. The fact is that Jesus asks of us what, in our natural state, we do not wish to give: *the totality of ourselves.* "Whoever finds (or holds on to) his life shall lose it...."

We think we are prepared to give ourselves to him, but then we awaken sometime later to discover that there was a part of us that had remained hidden, that was not surrendered. And the challenge begins once again, as he asks, "will you give that part of your newly discovered self to me?"

Who of us realizes the extent of our inner complexity? Saying yes to Jesus' call may in fact be a life-long process as, each day, we discover these hidden parts which are layer and layer deep within us. Each is its own fiefdom claiming independence from the Lordship of Christ. Each bitterly defends itself, and some of these parts do not give up without a struggle.

Yet we must bring these deeper parts to the cross. And when we offer them up to God, he will recreate them and give them back (the life lost is now found) to reflect his honor and our discipleship.

❧

So subtle is self that scarcely anyone is conscious of its presence. Because man is born a rebel, he is unaware that he is one. His constant assertion of self, as far as he thinks of it at all, appears to him a perfectly normal thing. He is willing to share himself, sometimes even to sacrifice himself for a desired end, but never to dethrone himself. No matter how far down the scale of social acceptance he may slide, he is still in his own eyes a king on a throne, and no one, not even God, can take that throne from him.

A.W. TOZER

"Anyone who loves his father or mother more than me is not worthy of me; anyone who loves his son or daughter more than me is not worthy of me; and anyone who does not take his cross and follow me is not worthy of me. Whoever finds his life will lose it, and whoever loses his life for my sake will find it."

MATTHEW 10:37-39

~ 89 ~

Do not turn a deaf ear to me.

Some of the spiritual masters referred to it as *the dark night of the soul.* They were thinking of times when it seemed as if God had deliberately withdrawn his presence. That there was no sense of guidance, power, assurance, calmness of heart. He simply wasn't there! Or at least not as they had come to know his presence.

No one knew a darker night of the soul than the Savior when he hung on the cross and cried out, "My God, why have you forsaken me?" Having known a perfect intimacy with his Father, he now knew the exact opposite: the infinite distance created by the sins of the world he was bearing.

We too have known dark nights of the soul. From previous moments when we felt the ecstasy of his presence to a moment when we feel the dread of his absence. Are we being tested? Is God expressing disappointment in us? Is it only our imaginations? Temptation?

"Praise be to the Lord, for he has heard my cry for mercy," the psalmist finally cries out. He reflects the assurance in the heart of Job who said while in extreme suffering, "Though he slay me, yet will I hope in him..." These are men of God who knew enough not to trust their feelings and their doubts. Even if it was a time of maximum darkness, even if every bit of their being told them that they were alone, something else deep within the heart was resilient enough to know: *he is there, and he will not be silent.*

❧

Oswald Chambers once asked, "Am I close enough to God to feel secure when he is silent?"

I plead with you to help me, Lord, for you are my Rock of safety. If you refuse to answer me, I might as well give up and die. Lord, I lift my hands to heaven and implore your help. Oh, listen to my cry.

PSALM 28:1-2, TLB

~ 90 ~

"The God we serve is able to save us."

Around the world today there are men and women who are
followers of the Lord who are well acquainted with the modern equivalent of Nebuchadnezzar's blazing furnace. For
some the furnace is a prison; for others it's the experience of
being beaten or tortured. There are other versions of the
furnace: separation from families, destruction of homes,
exile from one's community. Don't overlook the horror of
living in perpetual fear. Not a few in this century have died,
the victims of unspeakable atrocities. We dare not forget to
pray for our brothers and sisters of the persecuted church
who suffer so.

Among those of us who live in the west, persecution may
mean something different, much more subtle. While we, too,
sometimes face opposition when we identify with Christ and
his way, our "blazing furnace" is more likely to take the form
of loss of friends, threat to career advancement, a bit of
ridicule, and possible ostracism from mainline society. Never
a happy experience, of course, but hardly comparable to
what others are encountering.

When confronted with a furnace-like event, many have
reported experiences similar to that about which Shadrach,
Meshach, and Abednego spoke. They tell of a special sense
of heavenly presence, messages of assurance which go
straight to the heart, the strange supply of resources of
strength and wisdom for which there is no explanation.

We ought never to come to God's presence without inter-
ceding for persecuted Christians. Additionally, it might be

wise to read every Scripture and pray every prayer with the thought in mind: how might this be useful to me if a day might come when I was faced with the open door of a "furnace"?

◈

Remember Thomas More? Meg, his beautiful daughter, begged him to save his life by renouncing an oath he had once made. All he had to do to save his skin was to go back on a vow. But to deny a vow is to deny oneself: "When a man takes an oath, Meg, he is holding his own self in his hand, like water. And if he opens his fingers then he needn't hope to find himself again."

LOUIS SMEDES,
RETELLING THE THEME FROM THE MAN FOR ALL SEASONS

Shadrach, Meshach, and Abednego replied, "O Nebuchadnezzar, we are not worried about what will happen to us. If we are thrown into the flaming furnace, our God is able to deliver us; and he will deliver us out of your hand, Your Majesty. But if he doesn't, please understand, sir, that even then we will never under any circumstance serve your gods or worship the golden statue you have erected."

DANIEL 3:16-18, TLB

~ *91* ~

Pray for each other.

We have little trouble with those parts of Scripture that invite us to confess our sins to God. This seems a private transaction that offers a minimum of embarrassment, at least the kind we feel when we have failed in front of others. Left to confess our sins only in personal prayer, we are less likely to feel the humiliation that comes when we acknowledge that we have fallen far short of the biblical standard.

But Scripture does not stop with a privatized confession of sin. It calls upon the follower of Christ to become candid about sin with his brothers and sisters. This, of course, is another story. Here is where humility begins.

When I open my darkened and sorrowful heart to my Christian friends, I must use plain, unvarnished words, not the slithery clichés that can mark a personal prayer. I must permit my friends to see a side of me that I would have preferred left unknown. And I cannot avoid the fact that I am risking the possibility that my friends will be unable to forgive, that they will hold my confession against me. These are matters that toughen the notion of confession.

But God has called the Christian community—his church—into being for such a time as this. He wills our fellowship to be such that we can hold one another accountable to higher ways. Ours is to be a fellowship where one can hear words of grace and hope from fellow sinners who recognize brokenness and affirm that God has forgiven. And ours is to be a fellowship that will grant new starts and offer second (and more) chances.

We must never settle for a community less than this.

❧

Considering that by-standers always spy some faults which we don't see ourselves, or at least are not so fully sensible of: there are many secret workings of corruption which escape our sight, and others only are sensible of: resolved therefore, that I will, if I can by any convenient means, learn what faults others find in me, or what things they see in me, that appear anyway blameworthy, unlovely or unbecoming.

JONATHAN EDWARDS

Is any one of you in trouble? He should pray. Is anyone happy? Let him sing songs of praise. Is any one of you sick? He should call the elders of the church to pray over him and anoint him with oil in the name of the Lord. And the prayer offered in faith will make the sick person well; the Lord will raise him up. If he has sinned, he will be forgiven. Therefore confess your sins to each other and pray for each other so that you may be healed. The prayer of a righteous man is powerful and effective.

JAMES 5:13-16

~ 92 ~

You may be able to stand your ground.

Who of us has not found ourselves in a sticky situation and asked, "How did I get here?" In a distracted moment we say something that brings dishonor to ourselves and to our Lord. In an attempt to cut a corner, we make a choice with humiliating consequences. In a moment of discouragement, fatigue, or anger, we jump from one thing to another, and now regret our choice. And we ask, "How did I get here?"

In moments of such confusion, our instinct may be to blame other people or untoward circumstances. The human heart (ever since Adam) has been anxious to shift the blame outward, beyond ourselves.

The first believers understood that we deal with adversities both from within and beyond. In the human heart is a disposition toward evil we must guard against and submit to the managing power of the Holy Spirit. In the larger world, temptation calls us away from the things God desires for us.

"Stand your ground..." the old apostle calls to us Christians. Using a military metaphor he presses the issue home again and again. Stand firm! Be alert. There is a spiritual battle for the high ground of every human heart.

❧

How did I get here? Somebody pushed me. Somebody must have set me off in this direction and clusters of other hands must have touched themselves to the controls at various times, for I would not have picked this way for the world.

JOSEPH HELLER

Last of all I want to remind you that your strength must come from the Lord's mighty power within you. Put on all of God's armor so that you will be able to stand safe against all strategies and tricks of Satan. For we are not fighting against people made of flesh and blood, but against persons without bodies—the evil rulers of the unseen world, those mighty satanic beings and great evil princes of darkness who rule this world; and against huge numbers of wicked spirits in the spirit world.

So use every piece of God's armor to resist the enemy whenever he attacks, and when it is all over, you will be standing up.

But to do this, you will need the strong belt of truth and breastplate of God's approval. Wear shoes that are able to speed you on as you preach the Good News of peace with God. In every battle you will need faith as your shield to stop the fiery arrows aimed at you by Satan. And you will need the helmet of salvation and the sword of the Spirit—which is the Word of God.

Pray all the time. Ask God for anything in line with the Holy Spirit's wishes. Plead with him, reminding him of your needs, and keep praying earnestly for all Christians everywhere. Pray for me, too, and ask God to give me the right words as I boldly tell others about the Lord, and as I explain to them that his salvation is for the Gentiles too. I am in chains now for preaching this message from God. But pray that I will keep on speaking out boldly for him even here in prison, as I should.

EPHESIANS 6:10-20, TLB

~ *93* ~

On that day you shall do no work.

Regardless of what we do in the course of our work, we can expect that we shall slowly lose more of the sense of the eternal as the weeks and days go by. Ever since Adam and Eve lost their garden privileges, humankind has been locked into a life that generates physical exhaustion and spiritual drain.

Only a regular renunciation, a strategic spiritual pause, will rectify this fatal difficulty. It is the purpose of Sabbath to restore what is lost. Knowing this, God observed the first Sabbath rest, not because he needed it (because his work is not exhausting) but because he sought to model what it would take for us to regain our inner spiritual composure.

Scripture does not compromise on this principle, although modern people do. And we do so at our own peril. Sabbath is (to borrow an old slogan) *the pause that refreshes.* In it we look backwards in order to "close the loop" on our days of labor. We own up to that which went wrong and give thanks for that which went right. In Sabbath we look upward and reaffirm our eternal ties to our Creator and to his blessed Son. And in Sabbath, we prayerfully plot the course for the near future as best we can while rededicating ourselves to faithful living.

❧

Maybe I have been living much too fast, too restlessly, too feverishly, forgetting to pay attention to what is happening here and now, right under my nose ... you have to be still and wait so that you can realize that God is not in the earthquake, the storm, or the lightening, but in the gentle breeze with which he touches your back.

HENRI J.M. NOUWEN

Remember the Sabbath day by keeping it holy.

EXODUS 20:8

It will be a sign between me and the Israelites forever, for in six days the Lord made the heavens and the earth, and on the seventh day he abstained from work and rested.

EXODUS 31:17

He went to Nazareth, where he had been brought up, and on the Sabbath day he went into the synagogue, as was his custom. And he stood up to read.

LUKE 4:16

~ 94 ~

Search me, O God, and know my heart.

It is not difficult to suspect that the writer of this psalm had an instinct to "cover up" when he failed. Each of us have defensive mechanisms to avoid having to repent and acknowledge ourselves as sinners. Denial, blaming others, offering excuses, trying to diminish the seriousness of what has been done. One detects that the psalmist tried all these and more.

In this psalm, he seems almost resentful at first that God would intrude upon his heart and upon his life. The reader is not sure that the writer *likes* the fact that God is aware of every jot and tittle of his life. Perhaps he wishes that God would stop looking.

But that is not to be. And the writer goes on to survey the majesty and wonder of God. And before he finishes he has changed his tune. Now he invites God to search the heart, to test it, to point up the wickedness there.

What is wrong with us? And how do we move from brokenness to wholeness? Good questions, these. The answers all begin with what the psalmist has written.

❧

Every serious thinker must ask and answer three fundamental questions:

1. What is wrong with us? With men? Women? Society? What is the nature of our alienation? Our disease?

2. What would we be like if we were whole? Healed? Actualized? If our potentiality was fulfilled?

3. How do we move from our condition of brokenness to wholeness? What are the means of healing?

PAUL TILLICH

> *If I say, "Surely the darkness will hide me*
> *and the light become night around me,"*
> *even the darkness will not be dark to you;*
> *the night will shine like the day,*
> *for darkness is as light to you.*

PSALM 139:11-12

~ 95 ~

O God ... earnestly I seek you.

Not every experience of devotional activity and not every attempt at worship will be equally satisfying. There will be moments when we think we cannot ascend higher or deeper into a sense of God's presence. But these moments are likely to be followed soon after by occasions of dryness, dullness, and lack of direction. In these times, we are caused to wonder whether we have made any progress at all, whether time spent in pursuit of his presence is wasted time.

The writer of this psalm, most likely David, had worshiped regularly when times were easier and challenges were few. But now he found himself in the wilderness. David was the object of a frantic chase, perhaps instigated by the fragmenting Saul, that could cost David his life.

Now with the pressure at its highest point, David craves a sense of God's assurance. He needs to know that he is not alone, that strength will be given, that his integrity is honored in heaven. Thus the psalmist cries after the Lord, and gains the confidence that he is heard.

It was in the routine days of his life, when David sought the Lord on a daily basis, that he learned to find the Lord. In those simpler days the patterns of spiritual seeking were created. Now in the difficult days, the practice pays off. God is not silent; David has been heard. And that is why in the best and the worst of days, we must press on similarly seeking the Lord.

❧

When we carry out our "religious duties" we are like people digging channels in a waterless land, in order that when at last the water comes, it may find them ready.... There are happy moments, even now, when a trickle creeps along the dry beds; and happy souls to whom this happens often.

C.S. LEWIS

> *O God, you are my God,*
> > *earnestly I seek you;*
> *my soul thirsts for you,*
> > *my body longs for you,*
> *in a dry and weary land*
> > *where there is no water.*

PSALM 63:1

~ 96 ~

Resist (the devil), standing firm in the faith.

Did we get it wrong? Weren't we taught that we fall at our weak points? Weren't we warned to shore-up our weaknesses of character and habit, our points of doubt and fear? Then how might it be possible that just when we have shown ourselves to be strongest, we might in fact be all the more vulnerable?

In the whole Bible, you would be hard pressed to find a stronger leader than Moses. This former prince of Egypt, who commanded an extraordinary number of ex-slaves and led them through the wilderness, had remarkable strength. When almost all others lost their trust in Jehovah, Moses carried on. When almost all others fell into complaining and whining, Moses endured. And when all others were prepared to dump him, Moses stood tall and refused to be intimidated.

At first, one finds it impossible to imagine that this man could fail at anything. But in his strongest moments, he failed to acknowledge and contain his anger, and it betrayed him. When he should have been at his highest point, he lost touch with himself and his true feelings and defied God's command.

A small thing, we are tempted to think. Why should Moses suffer such heavy consequences for a tiny misdeed when he had been so faithful up to that point? Perhaps one reason might be to warn all of us who come after, that we can never relax from spiritual alertness ... especially when things are going well. For then the enemy attacks—not from the weak side but the strong.

The Bible characters never fall on their weak points but on their strong ones; an unguarded strength is double weakness. It is in the afterpart of the day spiritually that we have to be alert.

OSWALD CHAMBERS

Cast all your anxiety on him because he cares for you.

Be self-controlled and alert. Your enemy the devil prowls around like a roaring lion looking for someone to devour. Resist him, standing firm in the faith, because you know that your brothers throughout the world are undergoing the same kind of sufferings.

1 PETER 5:7-9

~ 97 ~

Bring ... my scrolls, especially the parchments.

It should be no surprise that Paul would want someone to bring his books to the prison where he was incarcerated. His writings reflect a broad bandwidth of knowledge about past and present thinkers in the world of Greek philosophy. His way of presenting theological principles and perspectives displayed the knowledge of a man who never stopped growing intellectually. Clearly, Paul pursued a vigorous life of the mind. Intellectual growth was among his priorities.

The same could be said, if indeed it is necessary to do so, about other giants in the biblical family. That Moses was raised in the palace of the Egyptian pharaohs was no accident. Before he left Egypt to receive another kind of education, the learning of the spirit, he learned the intellectual craft and customs of his future enemy.

Solomon was a learned scholar on animals, birds, reptiles, and fish as well as plant life. He spoke three thousand proverbs and knew or had written more than a thousand songs.

Daniel, along with his comrades, was trained in the leadership academy of Babylonian royalty. His work for three pagan kings was quite prodigious. The man was utterly brilliant and wise.

These people are just some of the men and women of the Bible whose minds were alive and disciplined through reading, exposure to wise thinkers and leaders, and the massing of experiences in the larger world.

Their example sends a strong message. The Christian life

should include the way of the student. God delights in the person who regularly stretches his or her mind into a credible platform from which the way of Christ can be proclaimed.

ॐ

Reading maketh a full man; conference a ready man, and writing an exact man. Some books are to be tasted, others to be swallowed, and some few to be chewed and digested.

FRANCIS BACON

Do your best to come to me quickly. When you come, bring the cloak that I left with Carpus at Troas, and my scrolls, especially the parchments.

Alexander the metalworker did me a great deal of harm. The Lord will repay him for what he has done. You too should be on your guard against him, because he strongly opposed our message.

At my first defense, no one came to my support, but everyone deserted me. May it not be held against them. But the Lord stood at my side and gave me strength, so that through me the message might be fully proclaimed and all the Gentiles might hear it. And I was delivered from the lion's mouth. The Lord will rescue me from every evil attack and will bring me safely to his heavenly kingdom. To him be glory for ever and ever. Amen.

2 TIMOTHY 4:9, 13-18

~ 98 ~

I want you to know about the things that have happened to me...

St. Paul's sense of calling—to proclaim Christ and his saving power wherever his name had not been previously heard—was so consuming that immediate circumstances meant nothing to him. What we might think of as an unbridled catastrophe, Paul saw as an opportunity. Here, for example, are the words of a man who finds himself in jail and in a judicial process that just might eventuate in his execution.

Outraged? Complaining? Self-pitying? Not at all. If it was God's will that he be locked in a prison, Paul would make sure that every soldier and guard, every prisoner who shared the cell block, would hear his gospel. Everyone is aware, Paul writes, that my chains (read handcuffs) are not those of the emperor or the Roman government. These are the chains of Christ.

There is every reason to believe that scores of palace guards came to faith under the influence of the old prisoner. Doubtless many of them subsequently traveled to the far ends of the Empire, carrying the gospel with them. For this reason Paul accomplished more world evangelism from a prison cell (through other people) than he did when he was free to travel from town to town.

Paul's experience challenges the modern Christ-follower. What circumstances do we face today that we are tempted to call a catastrophe, but which are actually opportunities in waiting to put the love of Christ on display?

༄

It is the mark of a grown up man, as compared with a callow youth, that he finds his center of gravity wherever he happens to be at the moment, and however much he longs for the object of his desire, it cannot prevent him from staying at his post and doing his duty.

DIETRICH BONHOEFFER

It has become clear throughout the whole palace guard and to everyone else that I am in chains for Christ. Because of my chains, most of the brothers in the Lord have been encouraged to speak the word of God more courageously and fearlessly.

It is true that some preach Christ out of envy and rivalry, but others out of goodwill. The latter do so in love, knowing that I am put here for the defense of the gospel.... I eagerly expect and hope that I will in no way be ashamed, but will have sufficient courage so that now as always Christ will be exalted in my body, whether by life or by death. For to me, to live is Christ and to die is gain.

PHILIPPIANS 1:13-16, 20-21

~ 99 ~

Let the one who would be great be among you as a servant.

The Christian gospel stunned the world with a surprise. Its people were not interested in wealth or power. Because their Redeemer had engaged the world as a servant, they did too. "I have come among you as one who serves..." he had said.

The first disciples may have found it difficult to fathom that Jesus would not attempt to seize political or religious power at the right moment, as all the other would-be messiahs had. Doubtless Jesus' followers anticipated that there would come a time when their leader would live in a palace and would no longer say, "the son of man has no place to lay his head."

But he finally convinced them. He came as a servant. He lived as one, taught the servant lifestyle, and died a lowly death upon the cross. And then he asked all who identified with him to do the same.

The men and women down through the centuries to whom we look as extraordinary examples of the Christlike life all lived in the servant way. They began each day with a simple aspiration: *What can I do, what can I say, what can I give that will bring the love of Jesus more deeply into your life?*

❧

Said of the Salvation Army founder, William Booth, at his death: "He was a king among men as long as the world counts service as the badge of royalty."

They came to Capernaum. When he was in the house, he asked them, "What were you arguing about on the road?" But they kept quiet because on the way they had argued about who was the greatest.

Sitting down, Jesus called the Twelve and said, "If anyone wants to be first, he must be the very last, and the servant of all."

MARK 9:33-35

~ *100* ~

"The world was not worthy of them..."

From the earliest days of creation, when Abel was murdered for his faithfulness, there have been martyrs. We have only a fraction of all the names. An overwhelming number have died in obscurity, and only heaven has the complete directory.

These martyrs remind us that Christianity is, at its base, a suffering faith. Founded by one who willingly went to a cross on our behalf, the message of our faith has been spread by those willing to pay any price to bring the love of Christ to one more person. The intrinsic truth of the gospel has been vouched for by those who obediently laid down their lives, that the truth might not be compromised.

We would do well to begin each day contemplating the possibility that we, too, might be called on to make a similar sacrifice, asking ourselves if we are prepared, and praying for those who will face the sword. For in truth: there are martyrs everywhere today. We must be prepared to join their ranks.

❧

When James Chalmers was killed by cannibals on the Fly River in New Guinea, all of Victorian England was struck with horror. Bishop John Oxenham wrote of Chalmers:

> Greatheart is dead, they say!
> Nor dead, nor sleeping!
> He lives on!
> His name shall kindle
> Many a heart to equal flame!
> The fire he kindled shall
> Burn on and on
> Till all the darkness
> Of the lands be gone.
> And all the kingdoms of the earth be won.
>   And one!
> A soul so fiery sweet can never die
> But lives and loves and works though all
>   eternity.

Women received back their dead, raised to life again. Others were tortured and refused to be released, so that they might gain a better resurrection. Some faced jeers and flogging, while still others were chained and put in prison. They were stoned; they were sawed in two; they were put to death by the sword. They went about in sheepskins and goatskins, destitute, persecuted and mistreated—the world was not worthy of them. They wandered in deserts and mountains, and in caves and holes in the ground.

These were all commended for their faith, yet none of them received what had been promised. God had planned something better for us so that only together with us would they be made perfect.

HEBREWS 11:35-40

~ 101 ~

He put a new song in my mouth...

The pit of which the psalmist spoke was probably a field prison where an army kept captured soldiers. Prisoners were often left there to starve, to suffer from the weather, to die. There was only one way out of such a pit: someone had to reach down and lift the prisoner out.

Have we not all known private versions of such a pit? The feelings of being trapped and vulnerable, of shame and total helplessness? What else might one do except—as the psalmist did—to call upon the Lord? The wise of heart know that the Lord will not leave us in that pit one second longer than is necessary to build something of eternal value into our souls.

Then in a moment of his choosing (and his timing is always best), we will be lifted up and out to a firm place. We will be given a new song, the capacity to sing it, and an audience who will listen.

In such moments a melody of salvation will flow from our hearts, providing others with hope and direction. We will see them go away afterwards, humming the song we have sung. And we will have cause to say as we look back to the pit from which we were lifted, *perhaps it was worth it after all.*

∻

At times God puts us through the discipline of darkness to teach us to heed him. Song birds are taught to sing in the dark, and we are put into the shadow of God's hand until we learn to hear him.... Are you in the dark just now in your circumstances, or in your life with God? Then remain quiet ... darkness is the time to listen. When you are in the dark, listen, and God will give you a very precious message for someone else when you get into the light.

OSWALD CHAMBERS

> *I waited patiently for the Lord;*
> *he turned to me and heard my cry.*
> *He lifted me out of the slimy pit,*
> *out of the mud and mire;*
> *he set my feet on a rock*
> *and gave me a firm place to stand.*
> *He put a new song in my mouth,*
> *a hymn of praise to our God.*
> *Many will see and fear*
> *and put their trust in the Lord.*

PSALM 40:1-3

~ 102 ~

Christ Jesus came into the world to save sinners— of whom I am the worst.

Humility may be the chief of all the Christian virtues. Wherever Christianity spread in the world, this remarkable quality of spirit became the mark of all who followed the Lord.

Humility—the inner attitude that frees a person to take the lesser position, to put another first, to have no need to impress others, to resist controlling others or seizing power—does not come to someone in a moment. It is the result of years of emulating Christ, who never utilized the normal human ways of power to assert himself.

When slandered, he felt no need to defend himself. When shunned, he never tried to promote himself. Jesus had no need for publicity, no passion for connections in high places, no desire for the symbols of success. He loved the weak, the simple, and the ostracized. He craved seeing lives transformed, people built into towering figures of spiritual strength. And even when the crowds turned against him and rejoiced in his dying, he prayed forgiveness upon them.

This is humility. And it is the mark of the true and maturing Christian.

❧

I never recall a single remark, a single word or silence, a single look ... which would go to suggest that he felt his opinion was entitled to more respect than that of old friends.... I wonder how many famous men there have been of whom this could be truthfully said.

OWEN BARFIELD ON C.S. LEWIS

That is why I am suffering as I am. Yet I am not ashamed, because I know whom I have believed, and am convinced that he is able to guard what I have entrusted to him for that day.

What you heard from me, keep as the pattern of sound teaching, with faith and love in Christ Jesus. Guard the good deposit that was entrusted to you—guard it with the help of the Holy Spirit who lives in us.

2 TIMOTHY 1:12-14

~ 103 ~

They go from strength to strength.

It is said that Wesley traveled more than forty thousand miles in his lifetime ... on horseback. That he preached an average of five times a day. He launched one of the greatest movements—Methodism—in the history of Christianity. He laid the tracks for revival throughout the western world.

If you are curious to know the secret of this success, read his words again. He sought God's heart *before* he did anything else. The man or woman who goes out to preach or, if not a preacher, goes out to work in the marketplace or raise children or study for a degree is not in a different category. Start each day as Wesley began his, and the difference will show quite rapidly.

Perhaps few of us are ready for Wesley's hour. Start with ten minutes, then. Or twenty. God stands ready to hear our most infantile utterances. God stands ready to teach us how to move from the infantile to the mature. And he stands ready to fill any man or woman with kingdom productivity when we take the time to fill our souls as Wesley did.

❧

On the first page of John Wesley's diaries there was always written: I resolve, *Deo Juvante,* (1) to devote an hour morning and evening to private prayer, no pretence or excuse whatever. (2) To converse with God, no lightness....

> *Blessed are those who dwell in your house;*
> *they are ever praising you.*
> *Blessed are those whose strength is in you,*
> *who have set their hearts on pilgrimage.*

PSALM 84:4-5

~ 104 ~

My soul glorifies the Lord, and my spirit rejoices in God my Savior.

God formed us to appreciate beauty and excellence. Whether that beauty is a direct result of God's handiwork or the product of human endeavor—through music, perhaps, or some other artistic form—we may marvel that something could be done so well. The achievement of the great athlete, the breakthroughs of the scientist, and the healing art of a brilliant physician often cause us to raise the standard of our own aspirations a notch higher.

We do well, however, to reserve our ultimate recognition for the One who has made us, who has equipped and inspired people like ourselves to achieve these great accomplishments, who has graciously given us the capacity to revel in them. The great innovations and discoveries, remarkable achievements, and larger-than-life charisma are all part of God's permissive purpose. The scientist, the artist, the athlete, and all the rest do nothing that God has not provided the genius and strength to do.

Therefore before we exalt them, let us perfectly understand that God's hand is behind it all, and that he is the one most worthy of adulation. Then when we have celebrated his presence in it all, it may be appropriate to give applause to those who do nothing more than fit in with his eternal will.

❧

First of all, my child, think magnificently of God. Magnify His providence: adore His power: frequent His service: and pray to Him frequently and instantly. Bear Him always in your mind: teach your thoughts to reverence Him in every place, for there is no place where He is not. Therefore, my child, fear and worship, and love God; first and last, think magnificently of God.

PATERNUS TO HIS SON

And Mary said:
  "My soul glorifies the Lord
  and my spirit rejoices in God my Savior,
  for he has been mindful
  of the humble state of his servant.
  From now on all generations will
  call me blessed,
  for the Mighty One has done
  great things for me—
  holy is his name."

LUKE 1:46-49

~ 105 ~

I confess the sins...
we have committed against you.

There are moments in our lives when our conduct is so ignoble that the memory of it lives on and on. In quiet moments
we think back to that event when we embarrassed ourselves,
wounded others, and grieved the heart of God. A prayerful
confession of sin is not adequate to cleanse the memory.

Perhaps this is an indicator that further restitution is needed.
Sometimes we are being led by the Spirit to return to the
"scene of the crime" and offer an expression of sorrow and
confession to the one we offended. Perhaps there is need for
returning something taken that did not belong to us. A slan-
derous or harsh statement must be untangled. A disobedient
act must be acknowledged. A selfish act must be reversed.

If the Holy Spirit should indicate such a necessity, it is wise
for the Christ-follower to move with appropriate haste. A
freed-up heart awaits the one who is quick to acknowledge
his or her offenses and seek the blessing of the offended
one.

❧

On a visit to Litchfield late in life, (Samuel Johnson) was
absent the great part of a day. Pressed to say where he had
been, he reluctantly explained. Michael Johnson (his father)
had tried to supplement his little book business by using a stall
at Uttoxeter on market days. Confined to bed with illness, he

asked his son to attend the stall. But "my pride," said Johnson, "prevented me and I gave my father a refusal."

Now on a rainy day precisely fifty years later, Johnson— with the violent bending over backwards that was at times typical of him—had forced himself to perform, in a way still harder for his pride, what he had refused his helpless father. For he had taken a (coach) to Uttoxeter, "and going in the market at the time of high business, uncovered my head, and stood with it bare an hour before the stall which my father had formerly used, exposed to the sneers of the standers-by and the inclemency of the weather."

"O Lord God," I cried out; "O great and awesome God who keeps his promises and is so loving and kind to those who love and obey him! Hear my prayer! Listen carefully to what I say! Look down and see me praying night and day for your people Israel. I confess that we have sinned against you; yes, I and my people have committed the horrible sin of not obeying the commandments you gave us through your servant Moses. Oh, please remember what you told Moses! You said,

"'If you sin, I will scatter you among the nations; but if you return to me and obey my laws, even though you are exiled to the farthest corners of the universe, I will bring you back to Jerusalem. For Jerusalem is the place in which I have chosen to live.'

"We are your servants, the people you rescued by your great power. O Lord, please hear my prayer! Heed the prayers of those of us who delight to honor you. Please help me now as I go in and ask the king for a great favor—put it into his heart to be kind to me." (I was the king's cupbearer.)

NEHEMIAH 1:5-11, TLB

~ 106 ~

He chose David his servant and took him from the sheep pens...

If Jesus Christ is, as we believe, Lord over all creation, then we must address all things from the perspective of being caretakers of that which has been entrusted to us. This is a revolutionary idea. When it is grasped, it changes our entire view of work, of engagements with people, of the use of everything we have.

This orientation brings dignity to every task and every encounter. There are no insignificant people, no small tasks. We are challenged to think all things, do all things, value all things out of love for God. The criterion by which we must judge our work, as he judges it, is *faithfulness*.

Tending sheep was considered a despicable task by ancient people. Yet this is where David, Israel's great king, was trained. He had been faithful in obscurity, so God raised David to be the leader of the nation, a writer of great worship poetry, the prominent figure in the family line of our Lord.

❧

Everything was the same to him, every place, every task. The good Brother found God everywhere, as much while he was repairing shoes as while he was praying with the Community. He was not eager to go into retreat, for he found in his common tasks the same God to worship as in the depths of the deserts. His whole means of approach to God was to do all for the love of him, and so he was not concerned about that which claimed his attention, provided that he did it for God.

DESCRIPTION OF BROTHER LAWRENCE

He chose David his servant
and took him from the sheep pens;
from tending the sheep he brought him
to be the shepherd of his people Jacob,
of Israel his inheritance.
And David shepherded them with integrity of heart;
with skillful hands he led them.

PSALM 78:70-72

~ 107 ~

When he came to himself...

Biblical writers convey to us Jesus' story of the defiant and self-centered Prodigal Son in just a few sentences. But even an imaginative child can fill in the blanks of the missing details. We know the pattern all too well. We have seen versions of the story in people we know; we have seen the story in ourselves.

A young man leaves home, moving out on his own. At first he enjoys considerable attention from people who love the pleasure-based life. The story of the Prodigal Son reminds us it is possible to live an outwardly focused life if you have the resources. But how long can one live that way?

For this young man, everything appeared to work until the economic climate took a downward turn and he ran out of money. "Friends" disappeared and all means of generating income dissolved. Soon the one who had been the life of the party was found living with the pigs.

The earliest hearers of this story were Jews, and we know what people in that cultural and religious tradition thought of swine. Nothing more needed to be said to make the point: *he hit the bottom.* And yet, it is precisely at this stripped-down moment that the outwardly focused life changes to an inwardly focused one. "He came to himself..."

Suddenly this young man saw his inner spiritual condition with a clarity that had been missing for a long time. Every past choice, every person he had hurt or used, and every act of squandering trust came into full view. The result? *Repentance.* Soon this young man was on his way home.

❧

I began to keep my diary, hoping to find myself in everything exact and almost without fault. How surprised I was and ashamed when innumerable deficiencies and blots and corruption appeared.

HENRY VENN
EIGHTEENTH CENTURY PASTOR

When he came to his senses, he said, "How many of my father's hired men have food to spare, and here I am starving to death! I will set out and go back to my father and say to him: Father, I have sinned against heaven and against you. I am no longer worthy to be called your son; make me like one of your hired men." So he got up and went to his father.

LUKE 15:17-20A

~ 108 ~

Look, your house is left to you desolate...

He walked out! Jesus, unable to stand it any longer, turned his back on all that was religious and walked out. In common, ordinary language, his last words before he shocked both his friends and his critics with his dramatic gesture were, "keep your house; it's empty (of spirit) anyway" (my paraphrase).

We dote on those Scriptures in which Jesus is seen moving toward people, and we reason that, in the same way, he comes toward us. We think of him in his graciousness, and we make the assumption that he would never depart from us—even when we ignore God, defy him, betray him. He will always be there, we think (consciously or unconsciously). But these self-serving assumptions dull us to another part of the reality.

Is it possible to become so cold and so resistant to the love of Christ that, for all practical purposes, *he walks out on us*—as he did that on the temple crowd? There must be a place in our devotion to contemplate this possibility. Perhaps this is the only way that the hardened of heart can receive the message. *Jesus will not remain forever where he is not welcomed.*

If there is a time when he will stand at the door and knock, there must also be a time when he ceases the knocking for a while and sadly withdraws. It is a prudent thing to ask ourselves every day: *is he here, has he been welcomed, is he being properly honored as the supreme Guest?*

❧

I once saw in India a fort on a hill outside a city. It had been the center of the life of a city and of a native state—the center of a princely kingdom. But the life of the city had moved on past the fort and left it high and dry and irrelevant. But sentinels still stood at its locked doors, dressed in somewhat shabby but resplendent garments, holding imposing but irrelevant spears as they guarded dead issues and dead values and dead authority.

E.S. JONES

"O Jerusalem, Jerusalem, you who kill the prophets and stone those sent to you, how often I have longed to gather your children together, as a hen gathers her chicks under her wings, but you were not willing. Look, your house is left to you desolate. For I tell you, you will not see me again until you say, 'Blessed is he who comes in the name of the Lord.'"

Jesus left the temple and was walking away when his disciples came up to him to call his attention to its buildings. "Do you see all these things?" he asked. "I tell you the truth, not one stone here will be left on another; every one will be thrown down."

MATTHEW 23:37-24:2

~ 109 ~

"My ears had heard of you but now my eyes have seen you...."

It is among the most ancient of all stories. Job was a business-man, husband, and father, and was among the most honorable of men in his generation. He enjoyed not only the approval of his friends but of God himself. But something remained untested in Job's life. His faithfulness had to pass through the furnace of suffering.

We are spectators to Job's awesome journey through loss. Without any reasonable explanation, he finds himself stripped of virtually everything: his family, his wealth, his health. The man who had everything suddenly has nothing. Even God seems strangely distant.

If we stick with the story, we see Job struggle with unspeakable pain. His faith is stretched to the breaking point. Easy answers do not suffice. And, in the end, as far as we know, Job never does learn what all of this has meant. God simply comes to him and provides an awesome demonstration of his power. And Job humbly bows to that.

Our world hates suffering. Even more, it abhors unexplained suffering. But Job went through it, and in the end, he triumphed. God rewarded him and restored, even doubled, all that he'd lost. And he gave him the privilege of being a spiritual model for all of us.

❧

It is highly doubtful that God can use someone until he [or she] has hurt deeply.

A.W. TOZER

> *Then Job replied to the Lord:*
>   *"I know that you can do all things;*
>   *no plan of yours can be thwarted.*
>   *You asked, 'Who is this that obscures*
>   *my counsel without knowledge?'*
>   *Surely I spoke of things I did not understand,*
>   *things too wonderful for me to know."*

JOB 42:1-3

"There is no one on earth like him," [God said of Job.] "He is blameless and upright, a man who fears God and shuns evil."

JOB 1:8

~ 110 ~

His pride led to his downfall.

Uzziah was one of Israel's greatest kings. He ascended to the throne at the age of sixteen after his father was assassinated in a rebellion. For fifty years he ruled, and under his leadership Jerusalem was rebuilt, the Philistines (Israel's perennial enemy) were thrown back, the army was restructured and re-equipped, and his royal prestige was considerably enlarged.

In short, Uzziah was well on his way to becoming the best of the best in a line of kings. It is said that he sought God and was "instructed in the fear of God. As long as he sought the Lord, God gave him success."

But success was not enough for Uzziah. Whether from boredom or simple defiance, Uzziah became dissatisfied with the scope of his privilege and blessing. Pride captured his heart, and one fateful day he made the impulsive decision to play "priest" and burn his own incense on the altar. This was something even a king was forbidden to do, and, Scripture says, Azariah, the priest, and eighty other "courageous priests" confronted him and rebuked him. When he would not listen and persisted in his intention, God struck him with leprosy. He died in isolated disgrace.

The sin of pride is among the most common of all sins, but it is also among the deadliest. As the story of Uzziah reveals to us, pride can strike and paralyze the heart when we least expect it. One moment we may be engaged in some of our best and highest efforts—the next, unless we are vigilant, we may find ourselves spiritually hardened and drowning in conceit. This powerful warning is Uzziah's legacy to us.

❧

Success exposes a man to the pressures of people and thus tempts him to hold to his gains by means of fleshly methods and practices, and to let himself be ruled wholly by the dictatorial demands of incessant expansion. Success can go to my head, and will unless I remember that it is God who accomplishes the work, that he can continue to do so without my help, and that he will be able to make it without other means whenever he wants to cut me down to size.

CHARLES HADDON SPURGEON

But after Uzziah became powerful, his pride led to his downfall. He was unfaithful to the Lord his God, and entered the temple of the Lord to burn incense on the altar of incense. Azariah the priest with eighty other courageous priests of the Lord followed him in. They confronted him and said, "It is not right for you, Uzziah, to burn incense to the Lord.... Leave the sanctuary, for you have been unfaithful; and you will not be honored by the Lord God."

2 CHRONICLES 26:16-18

~ 111 ~

We always carry around in our body the death of Jesus.

Someone must have tried to tell Paul that the people of
Corinth would never follow after one who had died a criminal's death on a cross. It would be far better, he must have
been coached, if Paul would redo the story and fashion Jesus
into a noble hero, acceptable to the Corinthian mind. Then,
perhaps, Paul would have half a chance to sustain a new religious movement.

If someone tried to persuade Paul along these lines, they
clearly did not succeed. Wherever he went, Paul insisted on
preaching about the cross and telling the story of the Son of
God who gave himself in death that sins might be forgiven.
In spite of this unacceptable story—"foolishness to the
Gentiles"—St. Paul (directly and indirectly) planted new
communities of Christ-followers from one end of the empire
to the other.

Paul not only preached the death (and the resurrection)
of Christ. He *lived* it! He lived that death in the sense that he
was prepared to suffer to the ultimate at any moment for his
cause. And he lived that death in his willingness to serve people, go to prison if necessary, and give away all that he had.
"I know how to have everything; I know how to have nothing," he said.

Paul's model of living should speak to our lives. Are we
prepared to "carry around in our body the death of Jesus?"
Or are we reluctant? Do we find it easier to say pleasant

things, promise gifts and bonuses, appeal to egos and the need for well-being? Or are we prepared to speak candidly about the centrality of the cross and of the one who bore our sins in death—that we might then know the life of Jesus?

❧

Shall we beat a retreat and turn back from our high calling in Christ Jesus; or dare we advance at God's command in the face of the impossible?... Let us remind ourselves that the Great Commission was never qualified by clauses calling for advance only if funds were plentiful and no hardships or self-denial involved. On the contrary, we are told to expect tribulation and even persecution, but with it victory in Christ.

JOHN STAM

But we have this treasure in jars of clay to show that this all-surpassing power is from God and not from us. We are hard pressed on every side, but not crushed; perplexed, but not in despair; persecuted, but not abandoned; struck down, but not destroyed. We always carry around in our body the death of Jesus, so that the life of Jesus may also be revealed in our body. For we who are alive are always being given over to death for Jesus' sake, so that his life may be revealed in our mortal body. So then, death is at work in us, but life is at work in you.

2 CORINTHIANS 4:7-12

~ *112* ~

I can do all things through Christ.

Beware of religious political correctness. It leads to a suffo-
cating laziness that is unattractive and unworthy of Christ.
We must be cautious about slipping into a religion (for that
is what it should be called) of mere words and symbolic
actions. When right answers and correct gestures are all that
matters among people who claim Christ as Lord, we begin to
relate to one another simply by trading platitudes.

The man or woman who bathes the day in prayer will be
tough on self. We must push ourselves to think clearly, to
yield more fully the fruit of the Spirit, to say less and listen
more, to honor others before ourselves. These are some of
the qualities Jesus seeks to bring out in us. They come, first,
through prayer, then equipping ourselves through study and
reflection, and then determined action.

෨ඓ

Keep me, O Lord, from waxing mentally and spiritually dull and stupid. Help me to keep the physical, mental, and spiritual fiber of the athlete, of the man who denies himself daily and takes up his cross and follows Thee. Give me good success in my work, but hide pride from me. Save me from the self-complacency that so frequently accompanies success and prosperity. Save me from the spirit of sloth, of self-indulgence, as physical infirmities and decay creep upon me.

SAMUEL LOGAN BRENGLE

I thank Christ Jesus our Lord, who has given me strength, that he considered me faithful, appointing me to his service.

1 TIMOTHY 1:12

I know what it is to be in need, and I know what it is to have plenty. I have learned the secret of being content in any and every situation, whether well fed or hungry, whether living in plenty or in want. I can do everything through him who gives me strength.

PHILIPPIANS 4:12-13

~ 113 ~

Stretch out your hand.

All of us know the difference between "fast food" and a gour-
met dinner. The one may provide a momentary burst of
energy, the sense of a full stomach. But hunger will soon
return. The other, prepared perhaps by a Parisian chef, is
arranged on the plate much like a work of art, its portions
carefully selected to provide nutrition, its diverse tastes balanced to please the palate. Having partaken of such a meal,
it will be a long time before hunger sets in again.

Why do we settle for "fast worship" which leaves the soul
longing for something more? Why do we cheat ourselves by
settling for that which titillates the emotions and amuses the
mind ... but starves the heart? But even more important: why
do we offer the God of heaven and earth something so
cheap?

Prayers consisting of platitudes and easily predicted phrases,
tossed thoughtlessly into the air, will not satisfy God *or* us.
Nor will empty songs endlessly repeated. Neither will amusing talks by preachers who are more intent upon impressing
us with the turn of a phrase than leading us to feast upon
the majesty of Jesus.

Ask more of your worship experience. *Give* more to it. It is
an understatement to even say it: but *God deserves it.* And, secondly, we cannot survive spiritually without it.

๛

Before the missionaries came to (Hawaii), my people used to sit outside their temples for a long time meditating and preparing themselves before entering. Then they would virtually creep to the altar to offer their petitions and afterward would again sit a long time outside, this time to "breathe life" into their prayers. The Christians, when they came, just go up, uttered a few sentences, said AMEN and were done. For that reason my people called them "haoles, (people) without breath," or those who failed to breathe life into their prayers.

MADELINE L'ENGLE QUOTING A HAWAIIAN WOMAN

"And when you pray, do not be like the hypocrites, for they love to pray standing in the synagogues and on the street corners to be seen by men. I tell you the truth, they have received their reward in full. But when you pray, go into your room, close the door and pray to your Father, who is unseen. Then your Father, who sees what is done in secret, will reward you. And when you pray, do not keep babbling like pagans, for they think they will be heard because of their many words. Do not be like them, for your Father knows what you need before you ask him."

MATTHEW 6:5-8

~ 114 ~

I am not ashamed of the gospel, because it is the power of God.

Examine Paul's life and you will see a two-part strategy. He sought to travel to places where Christ's name had not been spoken. And he sought to enter cities that were points of central influence to the regions around them.

In his commitment to that second strategy, preaching the gospel in Rome became a major objective for the old apostle. Rome? The seat of governmental and military power for the entire known world? How could any one dare to think that the gospel could find a foothold in Rome? What audacity! What gave the man the courage to think so aggressively?

Answer: the gospel was power. It was, in Paul's eyes, a greater power than the military and political power structures that established the Roman empire. You can go only so far with military force. You can exert only so much influence through governmental structure. But you can reach the hearts of people with the gospel of Jesus Christ. Rome's power? Limited. Heaven's power? Unbounded!

And thus the great missionary prepared himself to invade Rome. And before he was finished, the church at Rome was in motion touching the world.

❦

In the old days, when much of the world was unexplored and unknown, and when many lands were lands of mystery, men drew their maps; and in the unknown places they wrote such things as "Here be dragons," "Here be burning, fiery sands." The Christian can take the map of life and write across every part of it, "Here is Christ."

WILLIAM BARCLAY

I long to see you so that I may impart to you some spiritual gift to make you strong—that is, that you and I may be mutually encouraged by each other's faith. I do not want you to be unaware, brothers, that I planned many times to come to you (but have been prevented from doing so until now) in order that I might have a harvest among you, just as I have had among the other Gentiles.

I am obligated both to Greeks and non-Greeks, both to the wise and the foolish. That is why I am so eager to preach the gospel also to you who are at Rome.

I am not ashamed of the gospel, because it is the power of God for the salvation of everyone who believes: first for the Jew, then for the Gentile. For in the gospel a righteousness from God is revealed, a righteousness that is by faith from first to last, just as it is written: "The righteous will live by faith."

ROMANS 1:11-17

~ *115* ~

Blessed are the merciful.

An alarming number of people perceive modern Christians as angry, arrogant, and exclusive. What have they seen that causes them to conclude that the Christian way is unappealing and unsatisfying?

This should be a cause for our repentance.

Jesus envisioned a culture whose way of life would reflect the heavenly lifestyle. People known for their passion for peace. People brimming in mercy for the sinner and for those who are weak. People whose hearts were reserved for attitudes and intentions which reflect the character of Christ. People genuinely grieved when they see evil succeed.

Understandably this kind of culture is rare indeed. And it does not survive for long unless it is renewed within the human heart and in the community of Christ-followers on a regular basis. God stands ready to empower those who seek after the merciful way ... who are prepared to offer themselves a living sacrifice. Jesus called such people *blessed*.

❧

When men are prepared to die for their ideas but not to kill for them, only then will they be able to say that they've laid the foundations for peace. But humanity is nowhere near that. There's a lot to be learned on the subject of loving.

MICHAEL QUOIST

Now when he saw the crowds, he went up on a mountainside and sat down. His disciples came to him, and he began to teach them, saying:

> *"Blessed are the poor in spirit,*
> *for theirs is the kingdom of heaven.*
> *Blessed are those who mourn,*
> *for they will be comforted.*
> *Blessed are the meek,*
> *for they will inherit the earth.*
> *Blessed are those who hunger and*
> *thirst for righteousness,*
> *for they will be filled.*
> *Blessed are the merciful,*
> *for they will be shown mercy.*
> *Blessed are the pure in heart,*
> *for they will see God.*
> *Blessed are the peacemakers,*
> *for they will be called the sons of God.*
> *Blessed are those who are*
> *persecuted because of righteousness,*
> *for theirs is the kingdom of heaven."*

MATTHEW 5:1-10

~ 116 ~

Do it all for the glory of God.

The Christian life is one in which every event is meant to point people in the direction of God. We are tempted to think that this means big events, powerful speakers, or great acts of charity. And yet, God delights in the simplest act that is done in his name.

An omelet turned in a pan for the love of God? Picking a straw off the floor? One might as well conclude that our Father enthusiastically rejoices when we voluntarily pick up strewn waste paper from the floor of a public toilet. Or when we offer assistance to a mother with small children who has too many packages to carry. Could God feel genuine pleasure when we honor the underpaid server in a restaurant with a generous tip? Does God find pleasure when we offer an employer a greater quantity and quality of work than what was paid for? Is time given in conversation with someone society chooses to ignore a gesture of love toward the One who has made us?

This is a thought worth more than a little attention: that heaven smiles more on the simple things done in his name than all the great ceremonies of worship done in the cathedral. "In as much as you have done it unto the least of these my brethren, you have done it unto me."

❦

I turn my little omelet in the pan for the love of God. When it is finished, if I have nothing to do, I prostrate myself on the ground and worship my God, who gave me this grace to make it, after which I arise happier than a king. When I can do nothing else, it is enough to have picked up a straw for the love of God.

BROTHER LAWRENCE

So whether you eat or drink or whatever you do, do it all for the glory of God. Do not cause anyone to stumble, whether Jews, Greeks or the church of God...

1 CORINTHIANS 10:31-32

~ 117 ~

Listen, listen to me.

Sooner or later we experience what it is like to be short-changed, cheated, "taken to the cleaners." Perhaps we purchase food that has gone bad, a car that is a "lemon," a product lacking all its parts. Or maybe we have paid for a service that is not given, or is done poorly. Fool me once: shame on you. Fool me twice: shame on me.

Israel was fooled again and again, according to Isaiah. In its stubbornness, it always assumed that it knew what was best when it came to religion. And it always ended up investing its spiritual capital in defects. As a result, Israel became a nation of people who forgot how to listen to God speak.

There is a lesson here for us. Are we also too busy, too arrogant, and too self-possessed to hear the voice of heaven speak? That is how, after all is said and done, the human soul becomes empty. For all our wealth, we have nothing that satisfies, nothing that fills.

Great spiritual issues never change, and this matter of listening is one of them. When we call out, as did Samuel, "Speak, Lord, your servant hears..." our souls come alive.

એન્ટ

I only wish I could find an institute that teaches people how to listen. After all, a good manager needs to listen at least as much as he needs to talk.

Lee Iacocca
FORMER Chrysler CEO

> *Why spend money on what is not bread,*
> *and your labor on what does not satisfy?*
> *Listen, listen to me, and eat what is good,*
> *and your soul will delight in the richest of*
>   *fare.*
> *Give ear and come to me;*
> *hear me, that your soul may live.*

Isaiah 55:2-3

~ 118 ~

Each of us should please his neighbor for his good, to build him up.

The biblical community was unlike anything the world had ever seen as it spread from town to town in apostolic days. It was a time when the weak were expected to fend for themselves. Sick and deformed babies were put out to die. The diseased were expected to beg in the streets. The defeated were enslaved, and the aged died soon after they ceased to be useful.

By blessing children, healing the sick, honoring women, and ennobling the obscure, even the Gentile, Jesus Christ modeled a new way. If the soul was important and if every person stood equal before God, then human beings had a different kind of obligation to one another. Care, support, generosity, edification: these were the hallmarks of this unique society. And that society grew swiftly.

The tides of human relationship reversed wherever Jesus' name was valued. Rather than take, the new way of life accentuated give. Husbands and wives became committed to each other's growth as women and men of godliness. The older became mentors to the younger. The more mature Christian became a source of wisdom for the new believer.

The type and quality of conversation changed. Believers rushed to the aid of one another in times of crisis. Those who had once been society's outcasts were treated with dignity. And a new movement became characterized by the word love.

The man or woman who walks with God longs for that to be true in today's community of believers.

❧

Such people do not want to bear another's burdens but his benefits; indeed they want only to be carried by everyone else, but they themselves want to carry no one.

LUTHER ON ROMANS 15:1

We who are strong ought to bear with the failings of the weak and not to please ourselves. Each of us should please his neighbor for his good, to build him up. For even Christ did not please himself but, as it is written: "The insults of those who insult you have fallen on me." For everything that was written in the past was written to teach us, so that through endurance and the encouragement of the Scriptures we might have hope.

May the God who gives endurance and encouragement give you a spirit of unity among yourselves as you follow Christ Jesus, so that with one heart and mouth you may glorify the God and Father of our Lord Jesus Christ.

ROMANS 15:1-6

~ 119 ~

His face was like the face of an angel.

It feels as if Stephen comes to us out of nowhere. A congregation gathers to consider a solution to a serious, potentially divisive problem. Out of the discussion comes a group of names we've never heard of before. These men will give a new kind of leadership to the community of Christ-followers. And one of them is Stephen.

Stephen appears to have had an administrative gift. But it is not long before we discover that he has other gifts also: preaching, prophecy, and—most importantly—mercy. One cannot listen to Stephen's prayer as he died, pleading for the forgiveness of his executioners, without concluding that this was a man of extraordinary grace.

We have only a short account of Stephen's life. But what we do know of him suggests a man always on the growing edge. Always pushing the envelope, as they say. He gave willingly whatever friend or enemy asked of him. In the process, he lost his life. Or, as one might more accurately say, he found it.

❧

When a person becomes aware of the impact he can have on other people, he is highly motivated to perform at his best. And he's highly sensitive to the prospects of failure.

Consequently, it's no longer important to promote yourself. The only thing that's important is whether or not you do the kind of job that's expected of you. There's a tremendous satisfaction in losing your own identity in something that is much more important than you are.

KINGMAN BREWSTER

Now Stephen, a man full of God's grace and power, did great wonders and miraculous signs among the people. Opposition arose, however, from the members of the Synagogue of the Freedmen (as it was called)—Jews of Cyrene and Alexandria as well as the provinces of Cilicia and Asia. These men began to argue with Stephen, but they could not stand up against his wisdom or the Spirit by whom he spoke.

Then they secretly persuaded some men to say, "We have heard Stephen speak words of blasphemy against Moses and against God."

So they stirred up the people and the elders and the teachers of the law. They seized Stephen and brought him before the Sanhedrin. They produced false witnesses, who testified, "This fellow never stops speaking against this holy place and against the law. For we have heard him say that this Jesus of Nazareth will destroy this place and change the customs Moses handed down to us."

All who were sitting in the Sanhedrin looked intently at Stephen, and they saw that his face was like the face of an angel.

ACTS 6:8-15

~ 120 ~

Keep watch! Keep watch! Watch!

Several times in the same discussion Jesus drives home one simple but profound theme to his disciples. Anticipation, expectancy. History is rising, he says, to a great crescendo: the moment when the Son of God shall return in power and in glory. Don't be unprepared, he warns, for that momentous event. Be ready to stand in his majestic presence.

As did the others, Simon Peter heard this warning. Perhaps he did not take it seriously at first. But later he would write to Christian churches and warn them that some would scoff at this great hope, claiming that history has been going on for a long time with no changes. Don't believe it, he would exclaim. "The Lord is not slow in keeping his promise.... He is patient ... not wanting anyone to perish.... But the day of the Lord will come ... and the earth and everything in it will be laid bare" (2 Pt 3:9-10).

Whether the believer plans to enjoy the world or to save it is of little matter if plans do not include the contingency that Christ may return today. The great early prayer, Maranatha! (come quickly Lord Jesus) should permeate our prayers. The thought should cross our minds with frequency: if he should come in his hour, am I ready for his appearance? When we see God, may our first instinct be that of adoration.

❧

I arise in the morning torn between a desire to improve (or save) the world and a desire to enjoy (or savor) it. This makes it hard to plan the day.

E.B. WHITE

"No one knows about that day or hour, not even the angels in heaven, nor the Son, but only the Father. Be on guard! Be alert! You do not know when that time will come. It's like a man going away: He leaves his house and puts his servants in charge, each with his assigned task, and tells the one at the door to keep watch.

"Therefore keep watch because you do not know when the owner of the house will come back—whether in the evening, or at midnight, or when the rooster crows, or at dawn. If he comes suddenly, do not let him find you sleeping. What I say to you, I say to everyone: 'Watch!'"

MARK 13:32-37